THE PASSIONATE
INTELLECT

THE PASSIONATE INTELLECT

Incarnational Humanism
and the Future of University Education

NORMAN KLASSEN
AND JENS ZIMMERMANN

Baker Academic
Grand Rapids, Michigan

To our children,
Aidan, Conor, Anika, Nicholas, and Benjamin,
and to the churches that nurtured us
when we were students

© 2006 by Norman Klassen and Jens Zimmermann

Published by Baker Academic
a division of Baker Publishing Group
P.O. Box 6287, Grand Rapids, MI 49516-6287
www.bakeracademic.com

Printed in the United States of America

Library of Congress Cataloging-in-Publication Data
Klassen, Norman, 1962–
     The passionate intellect : incarnational humanism and the future of university education / Norman Klassen and Jens Zimmermann.
          p.   cm.
     Includes bibliographical references and index.
     ISBN 10: 0-8010-2734-9 (pbk.)
     ISBN 978-0-8010-2734-5 (pbk.)
     1. Education, Humanistic—History. 2. Universities and colleges—Religion. 3. Education, Higher—Aims and objectives. I. Zimmermann, Jens, 1965–
II. Title.
LC1011.K58 2006
378.012—dc22   2006009884

CONTENTS

PREFACE

IN A RECENT NEWSPAPER ARTICLE headlined "Advice for the 21st-century Atheist," a university professor compared religion to a beautiful picture, and then wrote this: "The only mature attitude to religion is to see it for what it is—a kind of art, which only a child could mistake for reality, and which only a child would reject for being false."[1] Our book offers advice for the twenty-first-century Christian at university who actually does believe in the reality of the picture presented in Christianity. The students for whom we are writing may have encountered a version of the sentiment expressed above—that their belief betrays what at best can be called intellectual immaturity—and perceive its belittling, prejudicial character: "the *only* mature attitude . . ."; ". . . which only a *child* could mistake for reality." In fact, Christian belief seriously maintained is often considered anti-intellectual in the contemporary university, or at least a bias to be overcome. The students we wish to address are committed to the intellectual viability of their faith as part of their growth into maturity and are simultaneously convinced that they can thrive at university, learning from a variety of perspectives and contributing their own.

1. Dylan Evans, "Advice for the 21st-century Atheist," *The Guardian Weekly* (May 6–12, 2005), 6.

Such students are often beset by a different challenge as well, from conservative Christians suspicious of university education. Sometimes parents, relatives, well-meaning churchgoers, and pastors can subtly or not-so-subtly express the opinion that all you need to be truly spiritual is to read your Bible and find a good church. It is as though the life of the mind could be restricted to a minor activity undertaken in a small area with clear boundaries, or worse, that the mind is like a vestigial organ with no clear use for the Christian. Purveyors of this suspicious attitude, when they catch a whiff of arguments that are as pejorative as they are sophisticated, such as the advice to atheists above, consider such evidence as confirming their worst fears. It is not always easy for the Christian student committed to pursuing university education to know how to negotiate such concerns voiced from within the church.

This book offers resources for coping with these issues. The students we have in mind embrace the greater freedom and need for independent yet rigorous thinking at university as compared with high school or Sunday school. They also have confidence in their ability to function in society as young, independent adults. At the same time, they recognize that the stakes are high at this stage of their intellectual and spiritual formation. They aspire to combine a passion for learning and relevance with spiritual integrity. For this reason, some may have chosen to obtain their undergraduate education at a Christian liberal arts university. Others may have chosen to pursue their education at a so-called secular university, confident in their ability to parry intellectual prejudice and to find spiritual nourishment in that context but needing encouragement and support. Either way, Christians need resources to help them grow, succeed, and contribute intellectually at university.

We set the challenges confronting the Christian undergraduate (and others) in the framework of the identity crisis facing the contemporary university as an institution. The historical movement away from religion, which reached a watershed with what we will refer to as Enlightenment dualism, has contributed significantly to this crisis. This book traces the development of the institution of the university and the changing attitudes toward people of faith within it. It also points students to the rich intellectual resources of the Christian tradition to enable them to understand the purposes of a university education. This heritage is increasingly relevant to the broader milieu of the contemporary university, with its anxieties of identity, relevance, and long-term viability in a world of short-term contracts, downsizing, and a fee-for-service mentality. Not only can Christian students thrive at university, they can also contribute to the institution's vitality.

Thinking about the institution matters because knowledge always has a social dimension. We wish that someone had told us about this social dimension and the complexity of the university when we were undergraduates trying to find a way to make a decent contribution to society and pursue the life of the mind. This complex institution is part of your intellectual community. Churches and Christian support groups are right to emphasize to students the need for Christian community while they are at university. Although both of us can tell stories about well-meaning keepers of the faith skeptical of the impact of university education on our souls, we have fond memories of the churches and Christian saints who supported us. The church has always implicitly recognized the social dimension of knowledge. Knowledge is not simply acquired in a social environment; one's social network and circumstances shape knowledge and make it what it is. One's social context is like yeast kneaded through one's university education.

We encourage students to take seriously this social dimension to the acquisition of knowledge. It has an extraordinarily important role to play in your ability to be an engaged, resilient, and academically successful Christian undergraduate. The university as an institution is part of the social context for the knowledge you are acquiring and putting into use. Understanding something of its history and changing ideals will help you both to acquire knowledge and to strategize how to be in the world yet not of it as a university student.

Although this book is written for the Christian university student, it also serves as a guide to the intellectual culture of the modern university, including its history. By implication, we want to foster dialogue and trust between Christians and unbelievers on a wide range of intellectual issues. By its very nature, the book encourages dialogue between those who hold different perspectives. We hope to cultivate in students greater openness to the views of others, especially across the divide that separates Christians and non-Christians.

In encouraging dialogue and trust between Christians and non-Christians on the life of the mind in the environment of the university, we are navigating our way into treacherous waters. The intellectual historian R. W. Southern, who, like us, champions a link between Christianity, humanism, and the rise of universities in the West, issues a warning relevant to our desires for this book: "Those who attempt to give a rational account of any religion are likely to dissatisfy believers to almost precisely the same extent as they satisfy unbelievers, and they are not likely in the end to satisfy either side."[2] We console ourselves, however, that we are not trying to give a completely rational account of Christianity. Nor are we trying to talk anyone into switching sides.

Our goals are more modest: to suggest that solely rational accounts of anything, including university education, leave things out; and to remind students that the life of the mind and the life of faith are not polar opposites, as people in the West over the last three hundred years have, until recently, increasingly supposed. We hope that the burden of our argument will provide consolation for Christian undergraduates, point them in a direction where they might find common ground with some non-Christians, and fortify them with counterarguments against certain positions.

Implicitly, we may also challenge some Christians who have a bunker mentality in intellectual matters, either because they have no confidence that resources exist for challenging intellectual prejudice against faith, or because they loftily, and to our mind erroneously, reject both the principle of dialogue and any belief in the shared pursuit of knowledge.

One final prefatory note: we have written this book as theologically informed Christians with a deep commitment to humanism (a term defined and explored in depth in the following pages). We do not write as professional theologians or attempt to construct an argument narrowly theological in orientation. Our aim in this book is to couch certain Christian reflections in broad terms. For instance, the term "worldview" (also to be developed in the coming pages), though not exceedingly technical, has tended to find usage in a certain confessional framework, that of Reformed theology. Indeed, Reformed thinkers brought "worldview think-

2. R. W. Southern, *Scholastic Humanism and the Unification of Europe*, vol. 2, *The Heroic Age* (Cambridge, MA: Blackwell, 2001), 102.

ing" to prominence, especially for the Christian community. Yet the term has come into use in wider academic circles, sometimes (ironically) with quite different underlying assumptions. Our use of the term, though indebted to certain circles of Christian usage (to which we are grateful), reflects the influence of wider contemporary usage, rather than that of a narrowly defined theological tradition, upon the university. Our engagement of theology in general is likewise broadly intended.

Our hope is to create new refractions of perhaps familiar patterns of thought for Christian students in a wide range of disciplines and from a variety of Christian traditions, and even for some non-Christian students as well. The strategy of recombining the theological with the humanistic will, from certain perspectives, appear to suffer from distinct limitations. Such a risk is inherent, however, to the task we have set for ourselves. Whether this strategy works you shall have to decide for yourself.

The Passionate Intellect took shape in the context of our coteaching a first-year course on humanism and of reassessing the principles guiding our own research and teaching interests. The book was made possible in part by a Council of Christian Colleges & Universities Networking Grant. As the name suggests, this grant allowed us to gain the perspectives of several esteemed peers working in different fields (Tony Cummins, Alex Hawkins, Bruce Hindmarsh) and to have face-to-face conversations with highly influential scholars, including Simon Critchley, Rowan Williams, Reinhard Hütter, and Charles Taylor. All modeled intellectual generosity, collegiality, and frank clarity. We'd like to thank Simon especially in this regard. Thanks too to Peter Erb, who cajoled, encouraged, and counseled us in countless ways over the years. Chapter 10 in particular was shaped by these conversations. We also acknowledge a significant intellectual debt to N. T. Wright. Thanks also to Jim Kinney, Brian Bolger, and the anonymous readers for Baker Academic. Our thanks to the academic administration of Trinity Western University for providing support with sabbatical leaves and for the recognition of our efforts with a Dean's Innovative Teaching Award. Thanks to our colleagues both at TWU and at St Jerome's University for engaging our ideas, and to Deane Downey for his passion for interdisciplinarity. Above all, thanks to our students, who in many

different ways over the years have challenged us to sharpen our
ideas and to clarify what we think is at stake for them and for
ourselves in the university environment. We dedicate this book
to several prospective students in particular, our children Aidan,
Conor, Anika, Nicholas, and Benjamin, and to the churches that
nurtured us when we were students. Finally, thanks to our wives,
Anne Klassen and Sabine Zimmermann, for their encouragement,
support, and intellectual companionship.

N. K. and J. Z.
Feast of the Annunciation

INTRODUCTION

> "The university is in ruins: nonfunctional in the social arenas of the market and employment, lacking cultural substance or an end purpose of knowledge."
>
> Jean Baudrillard, *Simulacra and Simulation*

WHY DO YOU ATTEND A university, and what should you gain from an education there? These are the two most important questions to ask when you enroll. The answers seem easy. I am at university to receive the skills I need for the career I want. And there is nothing wrong with this response, except that it can be only a partial answer if we are talking about a university. Any apprenticeship or trade school can provide those skills. If university education is merely for job acquisition to get ahead in society, why not reduce all so-called higher education to technical schools and computer colleges? This indeed has become very much a possibility with contemporary universities.[1]

Until modern times, the university had a different purpose, one defined mainly by a humanistic outlook on life. According to a

1. In this book we consistently employ the term "university" rather than "college" to accentuate a contrast between the humanistic goals associated with an education in the liberal arts (university, higher, or liberal-arts education) on the one hand and the more narrowly utilitarian purposes of trade and technical schools or colleges on the other. See also 191n2.

humanistic ideal of learning, the university was less a place for acquiring job skills than for producing exemplary human beings, good citizens of character, wisdom, and discernment. When a seventeenth-century university professor had to explain to parents why they should afford their children a university education, he told them that learning, humanistic learning, is the first ingredient for a better society. Knowledge of the liberal arts and sciences, he argued, "can be acquired only with strong dedication of the mind, with long and late hours of application, with sweat, with persistent discipline, and with punctilious discipline." For him, "our peaceful society" and its fruits are "for the most part based on the cultivation of these studies."[2] Is such a view still tenable or even desirable? If not, what is the goal of your university experience?

Like other aspects of Western society, the university has lost its sense of purpose. One academic summarizes the institution's plight as "humanism betrayed."[3] This problem is related to the loss of holism, including the splitting of faith from reason, in the changing ideals of the university. We are convinced that the same development that has excluded belief from critical thinking is also responsible for the current disciplinary fragmentation of the university and for the confusion of many professors about their vocation. Alarmingly, you may encounter professors who do not know what they are doing in the lecture hall or why. During a workshop on educational ideals and goals at an academic conference on the history and function of the university, a senior professor admitted, "I have no idea why I teach what I teach." This frank confession by a professor in the humanities, someone who assigns texts, holds discussions, and issues grades for his students, is symptomatic of the larger crisis facing the university. There are many indications that the university has lost its bearings and is no longer aware of existing for any greater purpose other than perpetuating itself. Not all of these symptoms are immediately apparent when you arrive at university to obtain an education in order to embark on a chosen career. Nonetheless, the indications of a university in

2. Giambattista Vico, *On Humanistic Education (Six Inaugural Orations, 1699–1707)* (Ithaca, NY: Cornell University Press, 1993), 35.

3. Graham Good, *Humanism Betrayed: Theory, Ideology, and Culture in the Contemporary University* (Montreal: McGill-Queen's University Press, 2001).

crisis are all around and can be seen once we pay attention to the intellectual culture of the university as a whole.

For example, the fragmentation of academic disciplines is rather obvious. Although many universities still force students, especially in their undergraduate program, to take courses outside their subject area, the rationale is often very sketchy. Students often wonder why they should "waste" time on these deviations from their direct path toward a degree in their chosen discipline. Especially in so-called practical or professional programs, more humanistically oriented disciplines such as philosophy and literature—and even the scientific liberal arts, such as physics and pure mathematics—are poorly defended as necessary components of a complete education. Disciplinary fragmentation indicates the lack of an underlying shared foundation.

Another related symptom of the university's crisis is what has become known as the managerial university. Economic forces have conspired to transform the university into a business whose primary mandate is to satisfy the desires of students as its customers or clients and whose administrative structure reflects this purpose. There are advantages to this change. Many European universities, with their arrogant, inflexible bureaucracies and aloof, inaccessible professors, are in dire need of a restructuring toward a more student-oriented model. But you do well to resist the temptation of their opposite extreme in North American universities, with students setting expectations and norms for their education that are market-driven. Such a system undermines the very idea of education by suggesting that students already know what there is to learn. Regarding students as knowledgable clients may seem flattering to them at first but is counterproductive in the long run. The managerial university can thrive only where a common vision has disappeared.

The university's crisis stems from confusion about its role and function in society. You will not escape this problem of self-definition in either a Christian or a secular institution. All universities face this confusion. The Christian institution worries about how to maintain its distinctive character but in reality faces the much deeper challenge of convincing students and their parents that excellence may mean more than ensuring gainful employment for graduates with a touch of spiritual reflection on the side. Liberal arts programs in large secular universities have as hard a time defending their relevance in our society as they do in private Christian colleges. The divide separating the liberal arts from practical or applied disciplines contributes to the problem of self-definition and can create some unexpected allies among both Christians and non-Christians.

To say that disciplines need to work together and that education is more than mere skill acquisition fails, however, to explain toward what end the disciplines should work together and for what reason the undergraduate degree should produce intellectually well-rounded students. Could we find the answer by recovering the older humanistic ideals of university education, namely, that genuine dialogue between academic disciplines facilitates progress in knowledge and that well-rounded individuals are both better citizens and more adaptable employees? Although this answer is undoubtedly true, it still endorses our modern idea of efficiency, with education and knowledge serving as mere tools. Simply recovering humanism is not enough to address the current university crisis, although it would be a good start.

Yet there is a richer, deeper purpose for your university education, one we call incarnational humanism. Incarnational humanism allows us to recover the great humanistic ideals of the university's past within the context of incarnational theology: because Christ's incarnation affirms the dignity of nature and humanity, learning becomes valuable in itself as a celebration of God's creation and as a benefit for the improvement of society. To see this point, however, we have to become better acquainted with the humanistic heritage of university education, a heritage that reaches back to the Christian origins of the Western university.

Interpretive Frameworks, Humanism, and Moral Education

The historical development of the university can provide a guide for the Christian undergraduate student's expectations. Historically, the university acknowledged that we all have interpretive frameworks; it assumed the dignity of human nature and of nature and strove to provide a moral education that enhanced character formation. Viewing your university education in the context of the institution's historical development will encourage you to shape your expectations of what you should gain from attending lectures and obtaining degrees. Traditionally, students, parents, and professors have not viewed the university merely as a wealth creator. Instead universities were places for developing shapers of culture, agents for the improvement of society. For the Christian student, this should still be the goal of university education, but with a crucial difference. Your goal as a Christian student, regardless of whether you have chosen to attend a Christian or a secular university, should be based on the fact that Christians are supposed to be the paradigm for a new humanity founded by Christ and inaugurated by his resurrection from the dead, a decisive event signaling the reconciliation of humanity to God and anticipating the full redemption of God's creation.

Such a historical examination reveals a residual yearning in university education, rooted ultimately in the economy of Christianity: that beyond the university's important role of providing career options and job skills lies the mandate to critical reflection on what constitutes a good career and a good life. We can phrase this mandate in many other ways. We could say that the university is all about the love of wisdom, about the *philos* of *sophia*. If "philosophy" sounds too abstract to be a mandate (which it should not if it really is the love of wisdom), we might alternatively say that the goal of university education is worldview thinking: reflection on our understanding of the universe and our place and consequent role in it. Such thinking necessarily requires the participation of all the disciplines, the asking of all the questions, and the prudential application of proffered answers.

A worldview is an interpretive framework. It has been defined as the "set of fundamental beliefs through which we view the world and our calling and future in it."[4] Much more than merely a cognitive lens through which we view the world, a worldview is deeply rooted in our tradition, culture, time, and history. Christian and secular thinkers quite agree that "interpretation is not only pervasive but unavoidable" and that "without interpretation we human beings could not live in this world of ours, given how we experience it. We are consigned to be, or honoured with being,

4. James H. Olthuis, "On Worldviews," in *Stained Glass: Worldviews and Social Science*, ed. Paul A. Marshall, Saner Griffioen, and Richard J. Mouw (Lanham, MD: University Press of America, 1989), 32.

interpreting creatures."[5] <u>Interpretation</u> represents a limitation, on the one hand, and a responsibility, opportunity, and honor, on the other.

University education should help us reflect on and consciously shape our worldview, our interpretive framework. This task of critical self-reflection in light of past and present intellectual, sociopolitical, and environmental developments is perhaps the hardest task we can undertake. It differs categorically from the rote learning of high school and is especially difficult in times when pragmatic considerations are so predominant in education. Because interpretation is unavoidable, because we are interpretive beings, university education is primarily a call to self-knowledge. The challenge to know yourself is an ancient motto in academic culture. It stems from the very beginnings of human self-reflection in the Greek tradition, and it is the <u>hallmark of university education</u> stamped by the impress of humanism.

This brings us to the central argument of this book: that your <u>Christianity is compatible with humanism.</u> When we look at the origin and historical development of universities, humanism emerges as the governing principle explaining their purpose, and its recovery is crucial for the healthy future of university education. It is a project to which Christians who believe in the life of the mind can enthusiastically devote themselves.

What is humanism? In the broadest sense, humanism indicates the spiritual quality of education. The well-known humanistic scholar Jaroslav Pelikan has summed up the driving motivation for higher education with the general axiom that "man does not live by bread alone." He explains that "the university has not discharged its intellectual and moral responsibility if, in its heroic achievement of attaining the possibility of putting bread on the table, it ignores this fundamental axiom . . . and both in its teaching and its research the modern secular university often ignores this at its peril."[6] The university can succumb to the temptation of thinking it has fulfilled its task by making it easier for its graduates to obtain well-paying jobs. The modern Christian university

---

5. Nicholas Wolterstorff, "The Importance of Hermeneutics for a Christian World View," in *Disciplining Hermeneutics: Interpretation in Christian Perspective*, ed. Roger Lundin (Grand Rapids: Eerdmans, 1997), 27.

6. Jaroslav Pelikan, *The Idea of the University: A Reexamination* (New Haven: Yale University Press, 1992), 18.

should heed the same warning. Even though Christian universities accept the idea that university education is much more than skill acquisition—that it includes character formation through intellectual training in a community of learning—this idea is often not reflected in its daily administrative and educational practices.

In a modern-day echo of the seventeenth-century professor cited earlier, Pelikan warns that "only the painstaking exercise of discipline illumined by imagination, and of imagination channeled by discipline, can lead to the rediscovery of an authentic humanism. Only such a humanism, in turn, will have something to say to those who, having finally found enough to eat, will recognize with shock that even in the midst of their famine they were yearning for life, not only for a living."[7] The following chapters will explore humanism more fully, but we can already hear from these two voices the insistence that humanism entails moral education. The notion of interpretive frameworks includes a moral dimension; moral education allows us to become more fully human by properly orienting us in this world.

The Fortunes of Humanism: From Holism to Dualism to Oblivion

Humanism went from a holistic beginning, which held together reason and faith, fact and value, to a more dualistic variety commonly termed secular scientific or Enlightenment humanism. Such dualistic humanism encouraged rigid divisions between reason and faith, fact and value, and the simplistic splitting up of other things that belong together, such as mind and body, thought and emotion.

Though dualistic, secular scientific humanism achieved some spectacular successes. It still underwrites many important values for university education. To picture the university as a place where we submit everything to the scrutiny of reason, as a place of freedom from authorities who would hamper our ability to question, as a place where freedom from tradition enables scientific and cultural innovations for the steady betterment of ourselves and society, as a place where reading great thinkers of the past helps us

7. Ibid.

to sharpen our judgments concerning present social and political philosophies—to think of the university in this way is to participate in the exhilarating vision that fueled the Enlightenment.

Enlightenment humanism, however, has suffered from two different shortcomings. Cut free from tradition and supposedly value-free, it has lacked the integrity to withstand the pressures of materialistic pragmatism. This humanism has found it difficult to resist the pressure to turn universities into job factories. It has thereby contributed to its own demise. Secondly, Enlightenment humanism has come under attack for its excessive confidence in human reason. Criticism of Enlightenment reason is a key feature of postmodernism. Postmodern thinkers would not welcome a utilitarian understanding of the university as a mere job factory, but they question the very possibility of humanism because they associate it with the Enlightenment's blinkered commitment to rationality.

Many postmodern thinkers are so disenchanted with the failed promises of the Enlightenment to deliver a better world on the basis of ideals such as truth, freedom, justice, love, and equality that they have become cynical about the pursuit of these ideals. As a result, wherever postmodernism has exerted a strong influence, former humanistic beliefs are no longer prominent. Instead of reason, one hears about power and ideology. Instead of logic and argument, one experiences political correctness. Many academics, indeed, denounce humanism altogether and explicitly teach antihumanism.

Recalling the origins and the development of the university as a humanistic institution will, it is hoped, convince you as a student that the highest goal and motivating force of university education is humanism in the modified sense suggested in this book and will open your eyes to humanism as the measure for your university experience. Humanism is the residual ideal that gave rise to many of the academic goals and structures you presently encounter in a university, secular or Christian. The question of humanism is all-important for understanding and confronting the current confusion about the purpose of university education. We will go beyond mere historical reconstruction, however, by outlining the recovery of an authentic humanism that encourages you to embrace the incarnation for the life of the mind. A Christian incarnational humanism will enable you to critique past efforts to marginalize

Christianity as well as present sub-Christian academic practices, structures, and expectations.

Postmodernism and Incarnational Humanism

Students should rightly expect professors to be able to defend their course content not on the basis of market value and sheer utility but in light of the greater aim of becoming more fully human. This humanism, however, cannot be merely a return to either secular humanism or even to Christian humanism based on dualism, for both share too many wrong assumptions—for instance, about the universality of reason, the independence of the human self, and the scientific nature of truth. An incarnational humanism, on the other hand, takes seriously *pre*modern commitments as well as *post*modern critiques of many past ideas about our humanity (especially those of the Enlightenment, which falls between the pre- and postmodern eras) but at the same time moves beyond the despairing, nihilistic implications of postmodernity. Only a biblically inspired, incarnational humanism can do this.

Postmodern thinkers have rediscovered one of the most important medieval (premodern) beliefs about knowledge—a notion gladly employed in this book: that understanding is always sought on the basis of "faith." If we are unabashed about linking the fate of the university to the Christian story, it is because one of the fundamental arguments here is that everyone has a faith: no one can bracket all of his or her assumptions and be governed strictly by reason at any given time. Even intellectuals stand in a tradition and accept certain things philosophically "on faith." One tradition or another limits your ability to think things through for yourself; the whole world is not available to you for a lab experiment. People who confess a faith, such as Christians, and those who deny a place for faith in the intellectual life, such as many nonbelievers, in fact have more in common than they may sometimes realize.

Admitting that all knowledge depends on faith commitments raises an inevitable question people often like to avoid under the pretense of tolerance, the question whether one faith is the right one. Enlightenment humanism developed out of just such a desire to overcome religious intolerance. Although we do not want to

sounds like [?] Mill

avoid this issue, its discussion could sideline the purpose of this book, which is to help Christian university students understand the purpose of their life as students, celebrate the life of the mind as an integral part of the Christian faith, and own their university education as an acceptable vocation in an institution that derived, after all, from a Christian understanding of the world.

Pointing to faith as a component of knowledge does not equate the university with the church. Even in the Middle Ages these two were distinguished from one another. However, observing the differences between the mandate of the university and that of the church, like the differences between the church and the state in general, does not mean that the secular university occupies some kind of neutral ground on which research is conducted free from subjective human elements of belief and cultural predispositions. In fact, it is the widespread recognition of the falseness of this view that, together with the hollowness of materialism, has ushered in the current crisis in higher education.

Fortunately, postmodern thinking has fatally undermined this unbiblical and inhuman idea of knowledge by re-establishing that all knowledge is contextual and interpretive. We agree (and think that Christians especially should agree) with postmodern critics who have insisted that Enlightenment humanism went too far. It did so by insisting on the freedom to question everything. This is not possible, for reasons (to be explored) understood by secular antihumanists and defenders of tradition alike. Enlightenment humanism came to misunderstand the nature and power of tradition. It also forgot that universities in the West received their start as Christian institutions. Christianity fostered humanism and is intrinsically committed to the full flourishing of human potentialities, not least the magnificent potentiality of the life of the mind. University education that tries to strip itself of Christianity, the church's commitment to the life of the mind as embodied in specific beliefs and practices, is doomed to failure. We have begun to see this failure with the assault on humanism.

By defining authentic humanism as Christian humanism, as faith that seeks understanding through intellectual labor, we situate ourselves precariously between two opposing camps. For many Christians, any humanism is synonymous with secular humanism, a self-centered, atheistic ideology that is openly hostile to Christianity and pitches itself as an alternative religion or a return to the values of pagan antiquity.[8] Admittedly, secular humanism's hostility to Christianity is partially justified by "dehumanizing versions of Christianity," which are nurtured by "the enforcing of substandard Christianity in homes, churches, schools, and communities,"[9] to say nothing of the sectarianism and infighting that has historically broken the unity of the church. Different versions of Christianity have inflicted enough emotional hurt to make many flinch from it altogether, and for good reasons.

This deeply entrenched distrust between the two camps will inevitably make very difficult the suggested recovery of humanism as a measure for university education and as a culture-shaping influence. To the Christian, the idea of Christian humanism as the driving force of university education may sound like a sellout to secular ideology, and to the secularist, Christian humanism may seem to condemn university education again to the invasive scrutiny and intellectual captivity of the Inquisition, with the Bible-thumping fundamentalist in the role of the grand inquisitor.

Yet we will have to undertake this tightrope walk—and argue that the student must similarly brave doing so—if we want to recover humanism as the guiding light for the university and for the character formation of future citizens and civic leaders. Although the differences between humanist schools as distinct movements in history are evident, we want to look beyond these differences (while acknowledging them) to the common themes in humanism insofar as they concern the nature of knowledge in university culture. All humanisms "share the desire of finding the human path to fulfillment and clearing away all that blocks it."[10] This desire should be common to all, even if the Christian ultimately has a different reference point for answering the questions of what it is to be most truly human and how we embody this purpose in our political systems and social practices.

Universities were originally Christian institutions, built on a holistically theistic, incarnational view of the world. And so, contrary to some current voices that clamor for a return to secular humanism as the foundation of university education, only a

8. J. I. Packer and Thomas Howard, *Christianity: The True Humanism* (Waco: World, 1985), 16.
9. Ibid., 18.
10. Ibid., 19.

theologically grounded humanism can take contemporary concerns seriously while at the same time enabling the renewal of the university's overall purpose as a place of cultural change. Learning and faith cannot be separated because learning is always the reflective unfolding of our belief about things. We can with good confidence return to the ancient theological conviction that all human knowledge is faith seeking understanding.

How does recovering humanism as the central idea of university education help the Christian student embarking on his or her course of studies? First, it can help you realize that a Christian university is not by definition inferior to a secular school. Often secular and Christian institutions appear to be completely different worlds, but they really should not be if humanism is the common goal of both. Therefore a student who transitions from a Christian school to a secular institution should not fear asking the same questions about frameworks.

This insight cuts both ways, of course. The Christian student has little reason for triumphalism because she or he should recognize that even a Christian education is not about receiving a coherent system of knowledge of absolute bullet-proof certainty that requires no further thinking. And so, recovering humanism can also help orient the Christian student by fostering an attitude of openness to the ideas and opinions of others, however unexpected the source of insight may be. Indeed, the student can initially greatly profit from postmodern insights into the social and interpretative dimensions of knowledge and understanding.

Conclusion

The university has become the most pervasive of Western institutions, the most dominant shaper of worldviews. Students often find that their worldview comes into focus at university. This is the place where they often decide, or in retrospect see themselves as having consciously decided, upon certain views. Their political views. Their understanding of the role of the arts in society. The possibility of attaining the good life. It is often the place where they lose their faith—or find one. From here men and women go on to influence their culture in small and large ways, turning their philosophy courses into screenplays, schooling their imagination to create great scientific and technological innovations, transforming co-op work experience into cutting-edge businesses, establishing the network of contacts that gives them lateral and upward mobility. They carry with them the swirl of ideas and attitudes they cultivated at university and tend to identify this potent mixture as "culture."

The years you spend at university are among the most important in your life. Above all else, university education should set you on the path of a new incarnational humanism, a lifelong pursuit of the good that is best described as faith seeking understanding. Christians helped to establish this goal for the university from the inception of the institution in the Middle Ages. But before turning to this history, let us address a basic question confronting many Christian students at university: do they belong there? That is, can they think in a manner befitting the institution?

Study Questions

1. Do you think the university is in crisis? If so, what signs have you noticed?
2. What do the authors mean by "interpretive frameworks"?
3. Do you think university education should have a moral dimension?
4. The authors tell the story of humanism. What is the plotline of this story?
5. What does postmodernism teach us about interpretation?
6. What is incarnational humanism? In what way do the authors think that postmodernism and incarnational thinking can go hand in hand?

CLEARING
THE GROUND

1

CAN CHRISTIANS THINK?

THIS CHAPTER PRESENTS TWO VERSIONS of the view that Christians are unfit for serious intellectual inquiry. This position represents an uncritical acceptance of a particular and not very ancient intellectual tradition. All thinking takes place within the framework of a tradition and a community. The church, for its part, needs to celebrate the place of the intellectual life as a vital part of Christian tradition. As a student, you can affirm your faith tradition as part of your intellectual makeup and should expect it to contribute to your intellectual growth.

Introduction

We want to challenge the very common assumption that Christian students and others who hold to a position of faith cannot do philosophy properly and, in essence, cannot think. We will explore the supposedly black-and-white contrast between the governing principles of the modern university, on the one hand, and dogma and authority, on the other. Christian principles in fact contribute to the intellectual life in ways the broader academic community now recognizes as being vitally important. Christian humility, though appearing to contradict healthy intellectual curiosity, encourages the pursuit of knowledge and beauty as a fundamental human activity.

The separation of religious commitment from the intellectual life in the university is misguided; to assume such a separation is to rely on an Enlightenment argument against thoughtful Christianity, a claim that is based on false ideas about objectivity. Let us throw down the gauntlet right here: to those who say, "Your faith is a crutch," we say, "Your assumption that, ultimately, Christians can't think is a crutch." — hmm?

The Argument That Christians Cannot Think

The opinion that Christians cannot think is widespread. Here are two examples of the prejudice, one from science and the other from philosophy, to which you could probably add stories from your own experience. The eminent American scientist Carl Sagan once said in his television series, *Cosmos*, "Science's only sacred truth is that there are no sacred truths."[1] This is a version of the idea that "Christians can't think" because Sagan intimates that belief holds certain things sacred whereas science holds nothing beyond hard-nosed inquiry.

Christians, like any other people with religious beliefs, do hold certain things sacred. We do not meddle with them but hold them in awe and respect. Usually, what we hold to be sacred we also consider mysterious in some way or another. The idea of mystery implies the acknowledgment of a limit to what we can understand: the Trinity, the incarnation, and the resurrection are sacred mysteries; the Bible, the institution of marriage, the celebration of the Lord's Supper are also commonly considered sacred.

These sacred mysteries Christians would call truths or sources of truth, but to a Christian, truth is first and foremost relational. It is not something one can hold at a distance and look at with supposed objectivity. Christians preeminently locate truth in a person: *Jesus* is the truth. Probably the most important implica-

1. In the book version, Sagan writes of science, "It has two rules. First: there are no sacred truths; all assumptions must be critically examined; arguments from authority are worthless. Second: whatever is inconsistent with the facts must be discarded or revised" (Carl Sagan, *Cosmos* [New York: Ballantine, 1980], 276).

tion of truth as being located in a person is that if a person who is true makes a promise, then you can count on this person to make good on his or her promises. For the Christian, truth has the character of trust. So the concept of truth is personal and the implication of this concept is relational. Indeed, the idea of a concept as something factual, clinical, or disembodied becomes secondary, if not contradictory. Sacred truths are not things like bits of unidentified compounds lying on the laboratory counter.

Some defenders of religion become preoccupied with the argument that there is an apparent contradiction in Sagan's statement (how can his statement be a "sacred truth" when there are no sacred truths?). Perhaps they make a valid point. But such an approach tends to put the discussion in the vacuum-sealed chamber of disembodied logic. To make such an argument is to shift attention away from truth as personal and relational, which is far and away the more important emphasis.

Disembodied truth, existing in a neutral nowhere, is not a biblical notion of truth. The Christian simply will not accept the idea that truth is disembodied or objective (belonging to the realm of objects), something that can be discovered without reference to the personal and relational. The Christian will want to say to someone such as Sagan, "I won't be bullied by your prescription of what the idea of truth has to be. Where did you get your definition from? What was your starting point?" The objections that Christians raise in the face of scientific assumptions are decidedly of a kind we now tend to classify as postmodern. They include an awareness of forever undisclosed assumptions and the exercise of power because a given discourse (in this case that of science) has acquired a degree of dominance that discourages the questioning of its basic presuppositions. This awareness is one reason this book will happily defend certain aspects of postmodernism. It hints at the inescapability of mystery.

What the scientist Carl Sagan says by way of slogan the philosopher Simon Critchley says in more leisurely fashion but with equally uncompromising conviction. We quote at length his argument that, basically, Christians cannot think:

> Heidegger notes in a striking remark from 1925, thinking of Nietzsche, "philosophical research is and remains atheism, which is why philosophy can allow itself the 'arrogance of thinking.'" Philosophy

is nothing if not arrogant, and furthermore it *should* be arrogant, a continual arrogation of the human voice. . . . So, in my view, philosophy—at least under modern conditions—is atheism, and to have an experience of faith would mean stopping doing philosophy . . . stopping immediately . . . right away.[2]

Critchley plays with the words "arrogant" and "arrogate." They share the same Latin root, *ad* + *rogare*, "to" + "ask." "Arrogant" is a word that entered the English vocabulary in the Middle Ages, around the same time that the universities were acquiring greater autonomy. The word "arrogant" has negative connotations in ordinary speech, but the philosopher Friedrich Nietzsche, then Martin Heidegger, and now Critchley flout the negativity to insist that this is a very important activity, "the arrogance of thinking." Critchley explains this phrase as "a continual arrogation of the human voice." The voice *asks*. If you do not ask the question, you will never find out the answer (something every professor wishes all students would realize). By referring to the *human* voice, Critchley posits a partial answer to an unstated question he is asking: what does it mean to be human? To be human is to ask questions, to think, to be inquisitive.

This is an interesting, plausible, and attractive suggestion. But although we very much agree with Critchley's definition of the human as arrogant, as a questioner, we do not see why rigorous human questioning has to exclude religious presuppositions. If, as already argued, all questioning originates from certain pre-suppositions, Critchley's insistence on philosophy as atheism is rather arbitrary, for it simply exchanges one set of assumptions for another.

Critchley's case for the arrogance of philosophy seems strangely blind to its own dependence on accepted authorities. We cannot help but notice the string of such authorities attached to the emphasis on the arrogance of thinking. Nietzsche and Heidegger have tremendous authoritative power in today's academy. A combination of appeal to authorities and of community building is at work here. *These activities—citing authorities and positioning oneself within a certain community—are as inevitable in the academy as they are in the church.* This does not mean that Critchley is not

---

2. Simon Critchley, *Very Little . . . Almost Nothing: Death, Philosophy, Literature* (New York: Routledge, 1997), 3 (emphasis his).

doing his homework and thinking things through for himself. He certainly does not cite these names without having read them, thought through their ideas, and positioned himself in critical relation to them. But the fact remains that he cites like-minded individuals who enjoy considerable intellectual clout these days.

Together with this particular philosophical tradition, Critchley assumes, first, that the self is the only possible starting point for asking questions and, second, that the philosopher's willingness to question everything requires a break with all positive religious traditions, including that of Christianity. Since Critchley's philosophical stance is a pervasive attitude in academic circles, it pays to examine these two prejudices more closely.

First, Critchley's starting point is indeed humanistic, for he champions the human quest for self-knowledge. In and of itself, Critchley's starting point for self-knowledge—the self who questions—honors the human and insists on the ethical nature of knowledge. Knowledge has a human quality in that it has to have meaning in relation to our entire existence. Critchley's atheism is problematic, however, because it makes extremely difficult an external measure for our self-knowledge, for ascertaining what it means to be human.

The Christian tradition, by contrast, has always insisted that genuine self-knowledge is impossible without an external measure of our humanity. For example, the Reformation theologian John Calvin wrote that "without knowledge of the self there is no knowledge of God . . . [and] without knowledge of God there is no knowledge of self."[3] Calvin acknowledged that knowledge about who we are must begin in some way with ourselves but requires at the same time an external source of knowledge. Only then does true self-knowledge become possible. Human existence has to be oriented toward an overall goal that goes beyond itself.

Philosophers such as Critchley realize that our desire to question and our thirst for knowledge require an ethical framework that transcends our self-interest. He realizes that the autonomous, iso-

3. John Calvin, *Institutes of the Christian Religion* (1559), ed. John T. McNeill, trans. Ford Lewis Battles, 2 vols. (Westminster: John Knox, 1960), 1.1.1–2. As McNeill points out, this hermeneutical circle is not original with Calvin but is mentioned already in Augustine and Thomas Aquinas. Augustine in his *Soliloquies* 1.2.7 states, "I desire to know God and the soul. Nothing more? Nothing whatever"; and in 2.2.1 Augustine prays, "Let me know myself, let me know you" (As cited in McNeill, 36n3).

lated self suggested by Enlightenment philosophy remains trapped in its subjectivist mental cage. Critchley, by contrast, insists on a socially constituted self. He is also fully aware that daring to think makes sense only when questions are directed by some kind of overall goal, but for him, this very goal smells too much of religion.

We find at the heart of Critchley's thought a typically post-modern dilemma: in the desire to protect self-knowledge from prefabricated, narrowing, and, indeed, oppressive stereotyping, postmodern thinkers forego *any* assertive or binding statements concerning human nature. And yet, to those who observe the debate from a theological or religious viewpoint, it seems quite apparent that the values at which all of these thinkers want to arrive (selflessness, the limits of reason, and the paramount importance of justice) ultimately drive them back to a concept of human dignity that the major religious traditions have always held.

Critchley's unease with positive religious assertions concerning self-knowledge is usually expressed in academic circles as a deep suspicion concerning "metaphysics." You do not have to move about in the academy for very long before you will be confronted with the ominous-sounding phrase "the death of metaphysics." Although there are more technical definitions of this term, it suffices to understand the term "metaphysics" as describing any theoretical construct that still attempts to judge human existence from an external point of reference outside time and place. Again, the reason for many academics' antipathy to such constructs is that the latter tend to become all-encompassing systems whose totalizing nature allows us to oppress undesired portions of humanity as inferior or unreasonable. Religious thinkers, including Christians, are included in the metaphysical camp, and so for one philosopher to call another a metaphysician comes as close to an insult as one can in an academic argument. To call someone a metaphysician is akin to calling him or her a Christian or religious person, a faulty thinker, who in the name of God suppresses freedom of thought and oppresses other people on the basis of absolute knowledge.

In fact, the intellectual tradition that has turned the label "metaphysics" into an insult has a long history of metaphysical mudslinging. The chain of consecutive upmanship resulting in the downfall of metaphysics goes something like this: Nietzsche dismantled Christianity and its moral God by demonstrating the silliness of religious belief in such things as God, the soul, and human freedom. Heidegger read Nietzsche and translated his "death of God" into the "death of metaphysics," by which he meant all constructs that indicate that one can judge human existence from an external point of reference outside time and human existence. Nietzsche did not quite obtain this radical stance, and so Heidegger called him "the last of the metaphysicians."

At that point, Heidegger himself appeared to be the only resolutely postmetaphysical thinker. But the philosopher Jacques Derrida, one of the French fathers of postmodernism, has since called Heidegger himself the last of the metaphysicians.[4] Recently the American atheistic philosopher Richard Rorty accused Derrida of using metaphysical arguments. For his part, Critchley has said the same of Rorty! And so it goes.

This internal divide over metaphysics in philosophical circles is more than mere entertainment because it points to the difficulty of dispensing with the religious. The religious or metaphysical is a specter that haunts these philosophers' daily work and is a useful weapon close at hand for them to use on one another. In fact, like Critchley himself, all philosophers who think seriously about the subject of our humanity come eventually to the conclusion that such reflection cannot remain confined to mere empirical observation but requires some kind of metaphysical claim, something that ensures our human dignity from some place that remains forever above our own experience and tells us what we ought to be like. So, ironically, good atheistic philosophy constantly circles about and tentatively plays with what religious traditions express positively: the need for reve-

4. Jacques Derrida, who died in October 2004, was a very influential contemporary French philosopher. He could be called the initiator of the postmodern movement known as deconstruction, at least as practiced in North American universities, although his ideas depend heavily on the thought of Nietzsche and Heidegger. Particularly in the 1970s and 1980s, Derrida was used to dismantle all sorts of belief structures, not just Christianity but traditional Marxism, structures that implied unfair power distribution, and uses of language that excluded as much as they included. Christianity was considered just a system of signs—liturgy, the Bible, communal practices—that could easily be dismantled and in fact contradicted itself internally, all of which showed its limitations as a human project.

lation, for a measure of our humanity that humanity itself has not produced.

We can also express this idea more generally by saying that self-knowledge requires transcendence, requires some greater whole to give meaning to each human experience. Even philosophers who realize this need, however, will not concede that any one religion or metaphysical system has such definite insight. The best that such philosophy can do is to admit this need without specifying its content.

Given this situation, is it realistic to claim that Christians cannot think? Is it indeed true that Christians cannot ask the hard questions because their inquiry moves already within the realm of belief and its suggested answers? As our brief discussion of this argument has shown, even those who make this claim do so on the basis of their own exclusionary assumptions. Furthermore, even within these assumptions, we have seen that a serious pursuit of self-knowledge, of the question of who we are, requires some kind of a religious construct that transcends our individual opinion about the essence of our humanity. Although it is true that certain branches of Christianity display strong anti-intellectual tendencies, this is not at all true for the Christian tradition as a whole. The idea that "Christians can't think" is a conclusion resting on highly questionable assumptions. When we examine these carefully, they often self-destruct. Because this point is so important and because it is in itself an exercise in worldview thinking, let us examine this claim in detail by investigating the sentiment in the thought of the influential German philosopher Martin Heidegger.

Christians cannot think, Heidegger claimed, because they have one ultimate foundation they dare not question—the existence of God. The philosopher, on the other hand, is not hampered by such ultimate limits, which is why the philosopher is the only one for whom nothing is sacred. Heidegger believed that real thinking has to begin with astonishment at the fact that things exist at all. Why is there something rather than nothing? For him, Christians have the ready answer, "Because God created," and therefore can never ask truly radical questions, can never experience real radical doubt, and hence cannot think. Heidegger's attitude also echoes an older Nietzschean idea that only a mentally strong and heroic individual can actually stomach this kind of thinking. Weak people, such as those who have faith and need a God whose existence solves all problems, are obviously unfit for rigorous thought. ~ I whole heartedly disagree

Many things are wrong with this view, which is based on a very thin understanding of Christianity. Who says, for example, that believing in God makes things easier? If we read the Bible carefully, we will see that the existence of God never made either existence or thought easier for anyone. Heidegger's claim that Christians cannot think is also contestable, however, on the grounds of his own argument: Heidegger believed strongly that our thinking grows out of our traditions and that we can never have a vantage point outside tradition. This also means that Heidegger's own definition of God as a crutch for the Christian was itself historically derived. Although Heidegger knew the medieval Christian tradition fairly well, he seems to have missed its most profound thinkers, whose writings testify to the depth and often agonized wrestling of intellects that were so profound precisely because they believed in God.

For a thinker who advocated the interpretive nature of truth and its dependence on tradition, Heidegger was lamentably inconsistent in his claim that Christians cannot think. To use Heidegger against Heidegger: thinking is always circular, moving from tradition toward the renewal of thought by its application to our current problems. To exclude the tradition of theology from this dynamic is fundamentally to deny the very nature of thinking as a historically conditioned activity.

Given this situation, is it realistic to claim that Christians cannot do philosophy or science or the arts properly, cannot be true to the spirit of these disciplines? The answer is that, indeed, Christians can and must think. Another way of confirming this answer is to return to the topic of tradition. Implicitly, Heidegger's argument that Christians cannot think still propagates the Enlightenment prejudice against tradition, as if someone coming from a religious tradition cannot think rigorously because he or she is hampered by faith commitments. The introduction above, however, has already stated that everyone has faith commitments. These commitments come not out of nowhere but are shaped by our respective traditions. In other words, contrary to the Enlightenment prejudice against traditions, we need to rehabilitate tradition as an important shaper of our worldviews.

Rehabilitating Tradition: Thinking as Individuals in Communities

A tension, even a fundamental conflict, remains: Is it always right to arrogate the human voice? Should philosophy be arrogant? For the Christian, this value is problematic. Religious people generally accept the authority of parents, pastor, government, teachers, and so on. Christians recognize the importance of obedience and stress the benefits of discipline. Independent thinking can represent a conflict with this set of values; it might indicate what the Bible calls a spirit of rebellion. Natural curiosity can tend in the same direction. In the Middle Ages, clerks referred to it as the vice of curiosity. Apparently a standard answer to the question "What was God doing before he created the world?" was, "He was preparing Hell for people who pry into mysteries."[5] The Christian church has tended to look on unrestrained curiosity as intellectual pride. The Christian witness has always spoken strongly against the sin of pride. It regularly heads lists of the seven deadly sins; it is presumed to have been the source of Lucifer's downfall. Much, of course, depends on what you understand to be "unrestrained" curiosity, but the fact remains that, for Christians, the intellectual life bumps up against the sin of pride.

On the other hand, the place of the individual and the need for weighing arguments for oneself are paramount. Refusing to go to church with one's parents can be the first sign of the work of the Holy Spirit in a person's life. At that moment, the individual begins to awaken to the need to take personal ownership of his or her beliefs. This process can take a very long time, has an uncertain outcome, and entails a great deal of intellectual work as one sifts through the various beliefs that have been taken simply at face value. This process often begins once the child has left the comforts of familiar surroundings and the security of home: at university.

Intellectually, individuality can blossom into the creative work of the philosopher, artist, or scientist. Originality is highly prized. The ability of the creative genius to think outside the box, to question the way it has always been done, and to present an alternative

---

5. Augustine, *Confessions* 11.12, trans. R. S. Pine-Coffin (New York: Penguin, 1988), 262. Augustine rejects this answer as frivolous because it does not take the questioner seriously.

vision has proven to be an attractive model for what kind of student the university should try to produce. This is a model indebted to certain tendencies within the Enlightenment paradigm. The genius was someone whose spirit was attuned to how the world really was and therefore had flashes of insight that were disconnected from any historical developments. The romantic genius was the proverbial rebel with a cause, a prophet of truth with unlimited confidence. Tradition and communal values were challenged as mere shackles to the freedom of the uniquely inspired genius. In modern society, we tend to make our way individually. We tend still to value very highly romantic elements of the Enlightenment in our aesthetic values and in the way we portray our scientific heroes.

In the twentieth century, however, growing appreciation of the complex influences of communities on individuals encouraged a revision in understanding how new knowledge, new theories, and new artistic works come into being. After a period in which the academy highly valued the individual's ability to look at existing ideas and dogmas from a distance and with a critical eye, we have come to appreciate the fact that none of us ever totally escapes social networks altogether.

Practically speaking, the inescapability of community means that Enlightenment "baddies" such as authority and dogma always accompany knowledge formation. One cannot escape them. This inevitability does not mean that one should strengthen a resolve to be forever on the run from all sources of tradition, such as the church. Rather it means that even though Western society has deposed the church as a significant authority, other forms of authority and dogma always fill the vacuum. A peer group, a set of social norms, a cultural context: these things always exert pressure on us. For instance, in any discipline there are usually two or three competing explanatory models. How an academic interprets data depends very much on which school of thought he or she belongs to. A school of thought is a community.

The field of medicine provides a good example of different scientific communities that need to cooperate and do not always do so. In that environment, doctors who are clinically trained are often perceived as having more authoritative status than people who work in the same fields but have nonmedical training, such as health economists or quality-of-life researchers. These days, the phenomenon of patient-directed care has arisen from the realization that many medical conditions include a host of different causal factors and treatment options. Individuals' responses to treatment can often depend on their sense of empowerment, their ability to be part of the process. And there often is not one single right treatment option. People with expertise in sociology, psychology, and statistics—all nonclinical specialties—are making an invaluable contribution to medicine's ability to deal with patients within the networks in which their lives are embedded. Different scientific communities are at work, and it is not always clear that they share a common goal, as debates over the value of quality of life and the sheer prolongation of life can quickly make clear.[6]

If the university provides some sort of social context anyway, and with it dogma and authority (however unstated these may be), then the concept of a Christian university can be seen simply as modeling the acknowledgment of just such a community context. Let us revisit the example above of the individual who decides to think through beliefs for himself or herself, often when leaving home and going off to university. This person enters into another community or set of communities when making this transition. The process of reevaluating beliefs happens in one context or another, however new, fragile, or provisional. A Christian university tries to minimize the shock by providing a sense of security and acceptance, a haven in which the individual can work through the questions and doubts that inevitably come over the horizon.

At least, that is what it should do. If Christian supporters betray too much anxiety and refuse to let the inquirer work through deep issues, then they have compromised the mandate of the modern university. In their (perhaps understandable) anxiety to provide for students an enclave secure from doubt, they also run the risk of betraying the faith. The faith invites careful scrutiny; Christ invites the doubting Thomas to see for himself his wounds; and God has infinite patience with the soul in its dark night, intellectual or otherwise. A Christian university that encourages the humanistic value of *Sapere aude!*—"Dare to think!"—can still be a faith-affirming institution. It can be the place where faculty can

6. For a discussion of the issues, see J. A. Muir Gray, "Postmodern Medicine," *Lancet* 354 (October 30, 1999), 1550–53.

model a combination of inquisitiveness, humility, and acceptance of mystery and where they can model having seen enough of their doubts reconciled with the faith that they have had their spirit of inquiry reinvigorated rather than lulled to sleep.

Thinking in the Church

One of the great benefits of community is the rigor required for exposing one's ideas to others and receiving the benefit of group insight, shared memory, and communal knowledge. This is a political process. The authority and the dogma of a community take shape over time; when we confront the church as individuals, it may seem as inflexible as granite, but it represents the collected wisdom of a community in its ongoing formation over time. For individuals in the process of acquiring a university education, a tradition or community provides a stable point of reference for assessing and assimilating the knowledge being acquired. Without it, one loses a valuable means of assessing one's ideas and insights.

In an individualistic framework, when faced with a set of doctrines, a student all too easily distances himself or herself from aspects that seem overly problematic or unpalatable. Individualism can reduce the level of demand placed on the individual, intellectual and otherwise. We declare to our friends that we are "basically Marxist," and have little difficulty hiding or shrugging off the contradictions in the way we assimilate our guiding principles. We tell ourselves (quite rightly, too) that no one has an utterly consistent philosophy of life and so we cannot be blamed. We all do this. Modern individualism makes it not only possible but imperative for us to do so, to fashion ourselves, to carve out our own identity. Yet this freedom can accommodate a sloppy inconsistency.

For a Christian, as paradoxical as this is, the church—that bastion of authority and dogma—can play a decisively enabling role in intellectual formation. For the intellectual pilgrim, the church provides a picture that is coherent but not complete. As the individual acquires new ideas and outlooks, she or he can try them on in the context of a specific community of a kind that is not readily available elsewhere. There is a degree of impersonality that is important, of the kind not available to one through family or friends. When we engage the church, we engage something much larger than ourselves. There is also a regularity to church life that makes it an ongoing dialogue partner, chafing and uncompromising though it may be. The church also represents a historical community, the thinking, practices, and memories of people who have coalesced around a cluster of sacred mysteries for thousands of years. The individual who interrogates the church with new questions and perspectives often finds that the questions are not always new, not always shocking. They have often been asked before. The individual, in her turn, is challenged by the church in ways a dilettante of the latest ism may never be held to account by any intellectual "community."

Conclusion

Although resentment against religion in general is, fortunately, growing less in our day and academia is beginning to realize that no one teaches from some kind of neutral ground, you may still quite often encounter the idea that Christians cannot think on account of their faith. This chapter, it is hoped, has given you enough material to show that this claim is specious. Christians can think; indeed they must think if they are to take seriously the biblical injunction always to be ready to explain their faith.

This chapter ends with a plea: Christians can think—please do! As a Christian student, please do not seek to avoid the hard work it takes to acquaint yourself with the political, sociological, philosophical, scientific, and religious ideas of our time. Christians face the double challenge of knowing their own faith well and also the worldviews of others. When they do so, they are in a formidable position to contribute to intellectual culture.

Humanism—a fundamental regard for the dignity of human beings and of nature (rather than the modern outlook that has set itself in opposition to Christianity)—has need of them. Belief in the dignity of humans has fallen upon hard times. It was a hallmark of the earliest European universities when they arose in the Middle Ages. The next chapter shows how Christianity enabled the development of a humanism that did not oppose faith to rational thought.

Study Questions

1. Have you ever experienced prejudice against your intellectual positions for whatever reason? For being a Christian?
2. What does Critchley mean when he says that "to have an experience of faith would mean stopping doing philosophy"?
3. What is the relationship between reason and tradition? Given the postmodern truth about interpretation, are reason and tradition strictly opposed to one another?
4. How can, does, and should the church preserve and stimulate genuine thinking?

The Story of Humanism from Its Holistic Medieval Beginnings to Postmodern Fragmentation

2

A HOLISTIC BEGINNING

Medieval Humanism

THIS CHAPTER TRACES THE CHRISTIAN impulse of openness to the world in the institution of the university, which
emerges from nonmonastic settings and is characterized by belief
in reason and the dignity of human nature and the natural world.
It introduces Thomas Aquinas as a holistic thinker able to balance
respect for reason and for the mysteries of revealed religion. It also
introduces Aristotle, a seminal figure of pagan antiquity, of whom
intellectuals in the medieval and early modern periods had strong
opinions, as this and the following chapter will show. To appreciate
the significance of Aquinas and Aristotle is to gain an understanding of important pillars in the development of university education
and, in Aquinas, of a model Christian attitude for approaching the
life of the mind and engaging the insights of unbelievers.

The Emergence of Medieval Universities

The modern university emerged in the first half of the twelfth
century, when the culture of learning shifted from a monastic set-

ting to one in the current of urban and secular affairs. The intellectual historian R. W. Southern had dubbed this era the heroic age of university education and humanism.[1] The change in setting evinced an important self-correction of medieval thought to avoid a one-sided spiritual or symbolist notion of knowledge. Although the best of monasticism evinces a holistic outlook, in this time period it had become easy to privilege a certain rather narrow understanding of religious learning. Although monastic education showed an interest in understanding and making sense of the universe, it proceeded by the centuries-old method of using symbolism to explain the significance of nature and natural phenomena. Using a tree as a symbol of the cross and of God's purposes in salvation history was much more important than trying to understand what a tree was, naturally speaking, and how it thrived.

This view of learning, however, was proving inadequate for a rapidly changing culture. Medieval western Europe was growing enormously in wealth, population, and power. This growth required new legal and administrative procedures as well as more clearly defined doctrines to govern the faith and practice of a predominantly Christian population. New places of learning were needed to provide these rules and to educate an increasing number of students who would furnish the burgeoning states with governing officials. The teachers of these new schools, first called "masters" and later "scholastics" or "schoolmen," were still clergy but were no longer bound by monastic rules. They were, rather, scholars *in saeculo*, in the world.

The Latin root of *saeculum* gives us our modern word "secular," but the teachers in the new schools were by no means against either God or the church as the modern word connotes. On the contrary, they embodied the mandate of Christianity to be in the world. The setting for their teaching was normally in the center of urban life rather than the cloistered monastery. They saw themselves as instruments of the church to provide doctrinal and legal rules for Christendom's beliefs and practices while retaining a degree of independence from papal authority. They were humanists in the simple and inclusive sense of teaching greater

---

1. R. W. Southern, *Scholastic Humanism and the Unification of Europe*, vol. 2, *The Heroic Age* (Cambridge, MA: Blackwell, 2001), 102. The following description is indebted to Southern's work.

respect for, and understanding of, God's creation and our place as humans in it.

The new methods of learning in these schools consisted in careful analysis rather than grand symbolism, and in a consideration of specific details rather than assuming that God's creation was mysterious and inexplicable. Christian secular schools, which were to become the first universities, emphasized the intrinsic value of God's creation and human nature. Things were interesting in their own right, not merely as signposts for a narrowly theological interpretation of reality. Christians realized that reason and the ability to understand nature were gifts from God that deserved to be explored and celebrated. Knowledge (the Latin word is *scientia*, from which we get the word "science") and the human ability to know became valuable in themselves. This was the birth of a genuine humanism, and it is a Christian humanism, a holistic view of reality as God's creation.

Southern explains this new combined interest in the dignity of human nature and the dignity of nature itself: "The two are linked together by indissoluble ties, and the power to recognize the grandeur and splendour of the universe is itself one of the greatest expressions of the grandeur and splendour of man."[2] The emphasis here is on the role of reason, the intelligibility of the universe, and a growing delight in the world for its own sake. Medieval confidence in reason and the intelligibility of the universe arose out of a fundamental commitment to the tenets of Christianity, now being worked out in a detailed and systematic way.

Medieval humanism transformed the tendency to overinterpret any object or historical event in disembodied, spiritual ways. But at the same time, the early history of these schools in the world demonstrates how difficult it is to retain a holistic view of things and how easy it is to slide into dualism. The new methods of learning, including rigorous systematization and logical abstraction, threatened to undermine the mystical elements of Christianity and tempted some to put too much confidence in the role of reason. (If postmodernism has preached the limits of reason, the church has recognized, at least since the rise of medieval universities, the challenges that accompany adherence to reason. Although postmodern thinkers tend not to qualify reason through any inten-

2. R. W. Southern, *Medieval Humanism* (New York: Harper & Row, 1970), 31.

tional respect for divine mysteries, their concerns are not always dissimilar to those who seek to combine faith and understanding, as we have seen.)

Perhaps the most celebrated case of a twelfth-century innovator in this regard was Abelard. His fame rests on two different dimensions to his life: a torrid love affair with a female student named Heloise and a refusal to bow intellectually to accepted authorities. In his approach to texts and metaphysical problems, Abelard emphasized the need for rules to govern the ways apparently contradictory authorities were reconciled. Abelard was a logician, and he sought to apply his expertise to the ways systematic theology might be undertaken.

Abelard insisted on applying his method to one of the central mysteries of Christianity, its doctrine of the Trinity. He believed that he could solve the mind-boggling mystery of God's nature by forcing the Trinity into the straitjacket of logical rules. He was bound to come to grief and by 1140 was condemned for denying the possibility of three persons of one essence.

The episode unfortunately has taken on the coloring of a battle between faith and reason. There are those who read Abelard's story as the beginning of a struggle for independent thought—that logic must be the final arbiter and that Abelard was exposing the impoverished thinking of the church. Are they correct? Can we not indeed detect a fundamental conflict in method between Abelard's no-holds-barred application of logic and his theological detractors? Does not Abelard's story confirm the suspicion that rigorous application of reason to religious belief always destroys faith and is thus feared by religious authorities?

Christian intellectuals did not, in fact, turn their backs on Abelard and his methods. On the contrary, the church recognized both the power and the limitations of his approach.[3] Within a generation

3. A similar recognition has been made of Heloise herself. Renowned for her learning even before she met Abelard, Heloise, after her tutelage from Abelard, went on to become the abbess of a religious house. Her letters to him reveal adoring deference to his brilliance but also the clear voice of someone who has worked out the political, social, and theological terrain for herself. As a faithful member of the church in a position of considerable influence and leadership, Heloise attempted to reconcile Abelard's strongly rationalistic bent with her duties to the church in an attitude that one historian simply calls a "mystery." This same historian, who set out to write about the medieval origins of humanism, confessed to being surprised by the importance

Abelard's dialectical method—in which he looked at issues by taking into consideration all the points for and against—influenced the writing of one of the most important church-sanctioned university textbooks of the Middle Ages. The case of Abelard takes us to one of the central concerns here. The logical extension of Abelard's predicament leads us to the uncompromising attitude articulated by the contemporary philosopher Simon Critchley, who has insisted that faith and philosophy can have nothing to do with one another (see chapter 1 above). Yet studied in context, the attitude of Abelard (like that of Heloise) reflects the complexity of belief and intellectual engagement in the time period.[4]

Reason has limitations, as is now widely recognized; mystery can never be dissolved entirely. The desire for complete clarity represents an Enlightenment goal never to be realized. Although, in the context of Enlightenment assumptions, faith has been largely considered inimical to thought, the life of the mind and the life of faith are far from being polar opposites. They certainly were not in medieval times. In fact, the twelfth century saw a bond created between the universities and the organized life of European society. Thinkers committed to the compatibility of reason and revelation turned their attention to developing a comprehensive outlook on life that took seriously this world and the affairs of human beings in it.

The work of Thomas Aquinas, a thirteenth-century friar and scholar, exemplifies this holism. Thomas did two things especially well, and they are surely related. First, he took seriously both God's word and God's world, following the example of the early scholastic humanists. Second, he embraced many of the insights of the ancient Greek (and therefore pagan) philosopher Aristotle (384–330 BC). Aquinas's openness to reason was such that he believed that insights could come from anywhere, that God's gifts could come to us from places we might not expect. Aquinas used Aristotle extensively for the development of his theology because he thought that since God is the Creator of

---

of Heloise to his story. "It was not difficult to foresee that I should have to deal with Abelard," he writes. "This indeed is what happened. On the other hand, I was very far from realizing that I should have to devote quite as much attention to Heloise as to Abelard himself." From Étienne Gilson, *Heloise and Abelard* (Ann Arbor: University of Michigan Press, 1960), 87.

4. Ibid., esp. 124–44.

nature, faith and reason are not opposed. And yet the teachings of Aristotle are often used to explain the beginning conflict of faith and reason. Which interpretation is true? Interpretation of the role of Aristotle in the development of the Western intellectual tradition can indicate different understandings of this heritage. The following will make clear that in Thomas Aquinas, one of the most influential medieval thinkers, the use of Aristotle modeled the integration of faith and reason.

Faith versus Reason? A Lesson from the Use of Aristotle in University Culture

A pagan Greek philosopher, Aristotle is often associated with a thoroughgoing naturalism and this-worldly attitude. Those who see a conflict between faith and reason often see in him a prime example of how the intellectual culture of the medieval universities was ultimately hostile to Christianity. According to this reading of history and humanism, Aristotle serves as an icon of secularity whose teachings are at war with Christianity. One recent introduction to medieval culture summarizes the influence of Aristotle on medieval thought by highlighting the contradictions between Aristotelian thought and Christianity:

> The recovery of an entire, coherent philosophical system from antiquity and the availability of [the Moslem philosopher] Averroës' commentaries created massive disruptions in the West's intellectual tradition. . . . Aristotle offered a method for investigation and a purpose for argument that differed entirely from the established Christian approach to problem solving and from its conception of the intellectual's task.[5]

This summary emphasizes disruption and opposition. In this common view among post-Enlightenment academics who champion the opposition of reason and faith, Aristotle made possible the development of science in the West. The rise of science, by implication, contradicts Christian belief. The author claims that the very principle of curiosity and its risks is contrary to the Christian

5. Hayden B. J. Maginnis, *The World of the Early Sienese Painter* (University Park: Pennsylvania State University Press, 2001), 3.

ethos.[6] He goes on to describe the implications of Aristotelianism for the universities:

> In the universities, [Aristotelianism] produced a class of intellectuals who saw themselves as philosophers and who came to ignore the contradictions between Aristotelianism and Christianity. Happy to admit their conclusions were often contrary to the faith, and to acknowledge that truths of the faith were truths indeed, they nonetheless maintained that philosophers' conclusions were also true. In effect, their position came frighteningly close to suggesting a system of double truth.[7]

In this interpretation, one could be forgiven for thinking that many medieval theologians were intellectual hypocrites. It is generally agreed that medieval universities were Christian institutions and theology was considered the "queen of the sciences." Yet, according to this view of the influence of Aristotle, the university gave rise to a class of intellectuals who lived with and even promoted two contradictory truths.

But this widespread interpretation of intellectual history is deeply flawed and reflects modern sentiments that distort our perceptions of medieval universities. The Christian belief in God's authorship of creation presupposes that the knowledge of nature and the use of reason cannot ultimately contradict the Christian faith. A prime example of this pattern is Aquinas.

Thomas Aquinas (1225–1274) did not share some modern historians' dim assessment of the relationship, or should we say the nonrelationship, between Aristotelianism and Christianity. He devoted much of his mature thought to reconciling pagan and Christian insights. His desire to integrate the world into his understanding of Christian vocation was evident early on. Like many people, Thomas had to endure pressure from his family when he was deciding on a career track. After he had finished his undergraduate education, studying the seven liberal arts of logic, grammar, rhetoric, arithmetic, geometry, music, and astronomy, the choice lay between becoming a monk and becoming a friar, and his choice reflects his view of university education.

6. Ibid., 4.
7. Ibid.

We have already examined how, a century earlier, education was shifting from a monastic to a secular setting. At the same time, new religious movements were developing that gave expression to different ways of conceiving the relationship between the church and the world. Thomas's wealthy and powerful family wanted him to become a monk and eventually an abbot, the head of a monastery. Monks and monasteries had a well-established place in the order of things: the vocation had a respectable and ancient pedigree and was carried out in the stable environment of well-endowed estates.

Thomas chose instead to become a friar, committed to preaching on the streets, living among the poor, and begging. One of the orders of friars, the Franciscans, would gain renown for producing a disproportionate number of early scientists. Thomas joined a group of friars called the Dominicans, who, though only recently formed, had already established important houses of study in Cologne and Paris. Although he had already encountered Aristotle as an undergraduate, he studied him in depth at Cologne. Thomas made it his business for the rest of his life to explain theology in terms amenable to Aristotelian philosophy. In this way, he pursued one of the chief objectives of all the orders of friars: to give expression to a practical Christianity oriented toward understanding and meeting the needs of the world.

Thomas's writings reflect his passions. One of his major works is a summary of church teaching for missionaries, the *Summa contra gentiles* (1259–1264) (*Summa against the Gentiles*); it defended the reasonableness of Christianity and the intrinsic relationship between reason and faith: "There are two ways of knowing what we hold to be true about God. There are some truths about God that exceed the capacity of human reason—for example the fact that God is three and one. There are also some truths that natural reason can attain. . . . Our intellect is led from the objects of the senses to the knowledge of the existence of God."[8] Thomas takes both reason and faith seriously. The organization of this work illustrates an important working principle. The first three parts deal with questions about God but approach them in terms of what is knowable by reason unaided by revelation. Thomas uses the Scriptures and church writings, but not as the basis of an argu-

8. Thomas Aquinas, *Summa contra gentiles* 1.3, in *St. Thomas Aquinas on Politics and Ethics*, ed. Paul E. Sigmund (New York: Norton, 1988), 3.

ment. Only in book 4 does he rely on revelation and ecclesiastical authority beyond reason to explain and explore the doctrines at the heart of Christianity: the Trinity, the incarnation, the resurrection, the sacraments. Aquinas used the same approach in what has become his best-known work, a summary of his teachings for university students, the *Summa theologica* (*Summa of Theology*). In both these works, as elsewhere in his writings, he defended the relationship between Aristotelianism and Christianity.[9]

The Limits of Reason: Thomas Aquinas's "Postmodern" Leanings

It is impossible here to explain in depth Thomas's intricate understanding of the relationship between reason and revelation. His main point, however, is that reason and revelation are not opposed but rather that natural reason points to revelation: "Since grace does not supplant nature, but perfects it, reason ought to be the servant of faith in the same way as the natural inclination of the will is the servant of charity."[10] Unlike Abelard, he maintained the view that reason is limited and cannot penetrate into the mysteries of God (such as the Trinity or the incarnation). Like Abelard, however, he saw that even in our understanding and articulation of these doctrines, we make use of reason. Thomas celebrated reason as God's gift but also recognized its limits.

Thomas found attractive the emphasis of Aristotle the pagan on the fact that *thinking happens within a context of other physical realities*. This situatedness draws attention to the limitations of reason. It is not self-contained or disembodied but in relation to, and in some ways dependent upon, other realities. Aristotelian thought helped Thomas work out the relationality of reason and our being in the world; it also helped Aquinas to articulate the relationality of reason and nonphysical realities, which we can generalize as the question of the relationship between reason and faith. He liked best

9. He is hard pressed at times to make the two compatible. For instance, Aristotle taught the eternality of matter, an idea that contradicts the Christian doctrine of creation. Thomas defends the doctrine but goes against other Christian thinkers by arguing that one cannot prove by reason alone that the world had a beginning in time.

10. Thomas Aquinas, *Summa theologica* Ia, q. 1, art. 8, in *On Nature and Grace*, trans. A. M. Fairweather (Philadelphia: Westminster, 1997), 46.

to think of the relationality of reason in two ways: in terms of the relationship between reason and institutions, especially the church, and in terms of the relationship between reason and love.

For Thomas, reason is embodied in institutions. If reason is not disembodied, then it ultimately cannot be entirely separated from political and social structures. Thinking does not happen in a vacuum. Traditions, embodied in institutions and political structures, structures of authority, necessarily interact with reason and help to shape it. In a famous move, Thomas simply accepts the Aristotelian assumption that humans are naturally social:

> But man is by nature a political and social animal. . . . [He] has a natural knowledge of what is necessary to his life only in a general way, using his reason to move from general principles to the knowledge of particular things that are necessary for human life. And it is not possible for one man to arrive at the knowledge of all these things through the use of his reason. Thus it is necessary for him to live in society so that one person can help another and different men can employ their reasons in different ways, one in medicine, and others in this or that endeavor. This is most clearly demonstrated by the fact that man uses words to communicate his thoughts fully to others.[11]

Reason, sociality, and language are all bound up with one another. Thomas gives a nice rationale for interdisciplinary studies, and with his emphasis on language Thomas anticipates a concern that will become even more central in the early modern period.

To return to the example of Abelard's insistence on reason, we can observe by contrast that Aquinas saw there could be no theoretical space for Abelard to undertake his thinking in a completely unfettered way. That one can point to the church interacting with an individual's thought is not in and of itself a bad thing. There will always be interaction between thinking individuals and institutions, and it will almost always be a two-way street of mutual influence and formation. One can only strive for a high degree of mutual charity, respect, humility, and willingness to learn.

Alasdair MacIntyre, a contemporary Catholic moral philosopher, explains the usefulness of the relationship between reason and social embodiment, especially for a robust understanding

---

11. Thomas Aquinas, *De regimine principum* (1265–1267) (*On Kingship* or *The Governance of Rulers*), in *Politics and Ethics*, 14–15.

of the importance of the church: "For the Platonist, as later for the Cartesian, the soul, preceding all bodily and social existence, must indeed possess an identity prior to all social roles; but for the Catholic Christian, as earlier for the Aristotelian, the body and the soul are not two linked substances. I am my body and my body is social, born to those parents in this community with a specific social identity."[12] Reason does not precede the body; it does not merely have implications for what we do with our bodies; rather, reason and embodiment are indistinguishable. When we argue for the role of faith and, indeed, of the church in one's intellectual formation and the fulfillment of one's academic vocation, as this book does, we are merely pursuing this understanding of the ways in which reason is limited by being in relation to other realities.

For Thomas, one also needs to recognize the relationality of reason and love. Learning was not simply an affair of the head but rather involved the whole of a person, including one's affections and desires: "The proper act of free-will is choice. . . . Now two things concur in choice: one on the part of the cognitive power, the other on the part of the appetitive power. . . . [Aristotle] inclines to its being an intellectual appetite when he describes choice as a desire proceeding from counsel."[13] The learner needs to have a receptive and responsive attitude. Like many others in the Middle Ages, Thomas conceived of the intellectual process as analogous to the union between lover and beloved, a union between the learning subject and the object of study.

The Latin word from which the word "study" derives, *studium*, can also be rendered "desire."[14] Learning engages the whole of

12. Alasdair MacIntyre, *After Virtue: A Study in Moral Theory*, 2nd ed. (Notre Dame, IN: University of Notre Dame Press, 1985), 172. These emphases on nature and politics very often go together in contemporary cultural inquiries. Hence titles such as Dolores Warwick Frese and Katherine O'Brien O'Keeffe, eds., *The Book and the Body* (Notre Dame, IN: University of Notre Dame Press, 1997); Miri Rubin, *Corpus Christi: The Eucharist in Late Medieval Culture* (New York: Cambridge University Press, 1991); and Elizabeth Alvilda Petroff, *Body and Soul: Essays on Medieval Women and Mysticism* (New York: Oxford University Press, 1994). In their different ways—and along with many others—these writers strive for a profoundly sociopolitical cultural situatedness along the lines outlined in the previous chapter.

13. Thomas Aquinas, *Summa theologica,* Ia, q. 83, art. 3, trans. Fathers of the English Dominican Province (Westminster: Christian Classics, 1981), 419–20.

14. For a discussion of medieval learning and spirituality in these terms, see Jean Leclercq, *The Love of Learning and the Desire for God: A Study of Monastic Cul-*

the subject, who is in relationship all the time. Rather than learning being preparatory, so that one can have a better relationship with the divine or with others (because one better understands physics or Shakespeare and has learned how to reconcile what one learned in class with what one reads in the Bible), the learning process *enacts* relationship; every act of study is an aspect of the comprehensive relationship we all have with God. For Thomas, because God upholds the world, there is no time at which we are altogether lacking a relationship with God. The truths of reason are to be found in a participatory, relational understanding of what occurs between subject and object. Learning in and of itself provides spiritual and moral formation.

Thomas found lots of support in Aristotle for this understanding of the learning process. The Greek philosopher exhibited just such a respect for, and relationship with, the world of objects around him. He did not look at objects in terms of their usefulness for someone or something else's ends; rather, he expressed unparalleled interest in the ends of the things themselves that he studied, whether in biology or political science. All things have a specific end and are not properly themselves until they have achieved this end. In his understanding of the cosmos, everything is in motion, put in motion by the First Mover and staying in motion until there is a perfect fulfilling of ends, resulting in perfect rest. The *desire* for this fulfillment of ends keeps things in motion; the universe operates on the principle of cosmic love.

Conclusion

Thomas adopted Aristotelian insights for Christian theology and for his understanding of learning. Because God's presence touches all things by God's sustaining power, when we learn about things, we also learn about God. The world is a text in the reading of which we learn about God and are, in a manner,

---

ture, trans. Catharine Misrahi, 2nd ed. (New York: Fordham, 1961). In Protestant evangelical circles, people also like to link learning and desire, but they do not tend to make the link in terms of the learner and the immediate object of study as itself involving a relationship. Rather, they invoke Philippians 4:8. Learning itself is not relational but rather an instrument to bring the individual into a closer personal relationship with God.

[handwritten: uh... that's why God gave us the Bible]

already transformed by tracing the handiwork of the divine Creator. This means that we can learn from anyone, Christian or not, who is serious about careful study of any aspect of God's creation. *[handwritten: ? How did we get this conc?]*

Thomas's appreciation and defense of Aristotle contributed enormously to the intellectual culture of the university in the Middle Ages. Fundamentally, he bolstered in Christian thought an attitude of openness and respect toward the surrounding world and toward others, ideas central to any definition of humanism. Universities in the Christian West flourished in this environment of inquiry. Nothing comes easily, of course, and Thomas found himself in many battles, defending Aristotelianism against both conservative skeptics and those willing to flout the boundaries of orthodoxy to embrace such teachings as the eternality of the created world. Aquinas would not become the official theologian of the Catholic Church until the nineteenth century, but within half a century of his death, he had been canonized a saint and his thought had made a massive imprint on the development of intellectual culture in Christendom.

Protestant evangelicals are attracted to the same insights. They often turn to thinkers such as G. K. Chesterton and C. S. Lewis for their apologetics. They find in these thinkers a particularly fulsome and far-reaching defense of the intellectual life and the contribution it can make to a vibrant spirituality. Chesterton was a Catholic thinker and ardent defender of Thomas, Lewis a High Anglican (one with close ties to the Catholic Church), a leading medievalist of his generation, and a strong believer in the rational defense of Christianity. Evangelicals would do well to ask themselves why they find these writers so attractive. The specific arguments that Protestant evangelicals import from their writings are nurtured in the soil of medieval Catholic thought, which emphasizes embodiment, desire, and socially connected rationality.[15] *[handwritten: ? see... I'm not weird]*

15. For some scholars, Thomas's way of conceiving this relationship is well suited to our contemporary environment, in which we have become aware of the limits of reason. At a time when some branches of philosophy have become disenchanted with their own tradition, especially since the Enlightenment, certain theologians have begun to press the relevance of this question whereas earlier it looked as if reason simply quashed revelation. Among Christians, Hans Urs von Balthasar, a prominent Catholic theologian, has argued that a proper understanding of the reason/revelation question could bring Catholics and Protestants closer together (*The Theology of Karl Barth,*

Aquinas's contribution to the development of humanism in the university is his holistic outlook on learning. He did not split faith and reason but opted for a reasonable faith, a worldview that appreciated creation for its own sake because it was permeated by the presence of God. Consequent developments in humanism, some of which further defined themselves in relation to Aristotle, could not achieve the same balance. We will examine these developments in the following chapters.

Study Questions

1. Do you think the church should play any role in university education?
2. According to R. W. Southern, what are the indissolubly linked emphases of medieval university education?
3. Describe the tension between reason and tradition in the outlook of Abelard and Aquinas.
4. What does it mean to say that reason is socially embodied?
5. What role do affections and desire play in your intellectual journey?

*I might enjoy Aquinas?...

trans. John Drury [New York: Holt, Rinehart and Winston, 1971]). He frames the issue in terms of the need for ecumenical dialogue and understanding.

3

LETTER AND SPIRIT

Literary Humanism

THIS CHAPTER TRACKS CHANGES IN humanism, and there-fore in university culture, from the Middle Ages to the early modern era. The development called literary humanism, which evinced a narrower emphasis on language, was both exciting and relevant to world affairs. During the era of literary humanism, Christians were very much at the heart of university innovations and advances; they helped bequeath a sensitivity to the embed-dedness of truth in language, a sensitivity that would be recovered only hundreds of years later. A rift developed, however, between what we call the arts and the sciences.

Introduction

After the achievement of a holistic Christian humanism in the Middle Ages, one of the markers of a shift from a medieval to a modern outlook was the development of other kinds of human-ism. These made important contributions to our understanding of university education but also contributed to the rise of modern dualism, a worldview that puts pressure on the suitability of a Christian student for hard-nosed intellectual inquiry. One of these kinds of humanism emphasized language (literary humanism), and a later correction privileged science (scientific humanism).

Whereas humanism in the twelfth century evinced a fresh interest in the details of life in this world and the theology of Thomas Aquinas provided a framework for passionate engagement in the life of the mind, the early modern period (1400–1600) was marked by attempts to distance contemporary culture from the medieval past. This in and of itself might not be a bad thing. Surely, if the new culture of learning was all that it was said to be and people took seriously the study of nature and of human nature, then they would discover things that caused them to change the way they thought about the world. Although this much is true, what seems to have happened is that learners lost sight of the goal of holding knowledge together. A rift developed between what we now think of as the arts and the sciences, between those who cared about language and those who cared about the properties of the physical world.

Literary Humanism Defined

Medieval humanism included respect for nature, for the dignity of human nature, and for the power of reason. It was open to all forms of *scientia*, or knowledge.[1] For many people today, the term "humanism" invokes the period of early modern or Renaissance humanism in contrast to the intellectual characteristics of the previous age. The idea of medieval humanism or of a heroic age of humanism in the Middle Ages may strike some as an anachronism. Southern calls the later kind of humanism that emerged in the Renaissance "literary" humanism. This humanism placed emphasis on the humane study of ancient literature and rhetoric, on urbanity, and on practical relevance as opposed to what it considered to be the self-contained formality and aridity of scholasticism: "The formal and systematic studies of the Middle Ages in scholastic theology, canon law and logic . . . were thought to

1. Although we normally think of the scientific revolution as happening much later, significant evidence points to a growing attitude in the Middle Ages that was genuinely empirical.

have excluded humanity, destroyed style, and to have dissociated scholarship from the affairs of the world and man."[2] Although literary humanism's emphasis on language presented a continuation of interest in the nature and function of language we find already in medieval times, literary humanists placed much more emphasis on ancient Greek and Roman sources to cultivate the mind.

Humanism of this kind looked back on the education of the past and saw it dominated by theology and canon law, irrespective of its home in the monasteries or the new schools in secular settings. Furthermore, literary humanism equated relevance with urbanity, with polished style rather than simply with systematic learning. In the twelfth century, people had adapted their learning in the schools to the needs of public life but not at all to the extent that this occurred in literary humanism. Here one can almost imagine a world in which style was everything.

Sometimes the reaction against medieval humanism is portrayed as a reaction against Christianity and the church on the part of worldly and arrogant intellectuals (whom some decry and others praise as "secular humanists"). Literary humanists, however, did not challenge Christianity from an atheistic perspective but rather disputed what they considered to be an ineffective, irrelevant preoccupation with arid logic, no matter where they found it. They would take one look at a textbook written in the style initiated by Abelard and call it *passé*. And they thought that a focus on logic and debates about natural science were irrelevant to daily life.

From a twenty-first-century perspective, this disdain for logic and prototypical sciences appears a bit odd. Today science looks like the more practical side of a university education, more likely to enable one to keep up with technological advances and more apt to garner the student a well-paying job. Yet in the era of literary humanism, the prospects for preferment looked better if one had a background in practical disciplines such as rhetoric, languages, and law. A closer examination shows that literary humanism un-

---

2. Southern, *Medieval Humanism*, 30. Charles G. Nauert, *Humanism and the Culture of Renaissance Europe* (New York: Cambridge University Press, 1995), 15, puts it this way: "Education in humanistic subjects appeared practical while education in logic and natural science, the dominant subjects in the medieval liberal-arts curriculum, seemed to breed idle debate about purely speculative issues that were totally useless for real life."

covered vital educational elements in its emphasis on the nature
and power of language, but it also encouraged a dualism that
favored one important aspect of our humanity over another. When
later thinkers reacted against it, they drove a wedge between the
arts and sciences more deeply still. As we see in the next section,
the Greek philosopher Aristotle continues to be a touchstone for
these developments.

Literary Humanism and Aristotle

Whereas holistic medieval humanism appreciated Aristotle for
his careful analysis of nature, literary humanists did not. To them,
Aristotle represented scholasticism, particularly scholastic methodology, and was antihumanistic.[3] Protestant theologians did not
like him either because they believed that Aristotelian vocabulary
could not do justice to the mysteries and spiritual dynamics of the
Christian faith. (Luther, for instance, called him a "buffoon.")

The reception of Aristotle in the Renaissance teaches us again
that intellectual history at this stage is not explicable in terms of
a conflict between Christians and non-Christians. Here was a
new movement in which all literary humanists (whether or not
they were theologians) shared a commitment to a fresh approach
to learning, inscribed in the phrase *ad fontes*, "to the founts," or
primary sources. This phrase encouraged students to consider texts
influential on Western culture, from Virgil to the Bible, for themselves rather than to rely on commentaries and learned authorities.
In the Middle Ages, many topics were discussed in Aristotelian
terms such as the "efficient cause" or the "final cause." When
literary humanists saw these categories, they saw the scholastic
urge to systematize; the categories themselves were proof positive

3. Frank James, "Peter Martyr Vermigli: At the Crossroads of Late Medieval
Scholasticism, Christian Humanism and Resurgent Augustinianism," in *Protestant
Scholasticism: Essays in Reassessment*, ed. Carl R. Trueman and R. Scott Clark (Ex-
eter, Eng.: Paternoster, 1999), 65–66; Nicholas Mann, "The Origins of Humanism,"
in *The Cambridge Companion to Renaissance Humanism*, ed. Jill Kraye (New York:
Cambridge University Press, 1996), 14 (on Petrarch and Aristotelians); Peter Mack,
"Humanist Rhetoric and Dialectic," in *Cambridge Companion*, ed. Kraye, 85–86 (on
Valla and Aristotelian dialectics). For a dissenting view expounding humanist Aristotelianism, see Jill Kraye, "Philologists and Philosophers," in *Cambridge Companion*,
ed. Kraye, 142–53.

that the writer had not drunk at the founts for him- or herself. The Aristotelian categories indicated slavish obedience to received tradition and a small-minded reluctance to think for oneself.

The literary humanists exulted in the freedom and responsibility of thinking for oneself. To do so required courage and tenacity, the intellectual prowess to learn the necessary languages, and connections to those among whom the manuscripts were circulating. This activity could include women. Based on his humanist belief in the universality of reason, Sir Thomas More gave his daughter Margaret Roper More the tools of linguistic competence and independent thought that enabled her to participate vigorously in the intellectual debates of her day. From time to time, women in the premodern and early modern periods pressed the point. Writing in the seventeenth century, royal tutor Bathsua Makin appealed to the universality of reason and the desire to learn to argue for women's access to education:

> Had God intended Women only as finer sort of Cattle, he would not have made them reasonable. . . . Seeing Nature produces Women of such excellent Parts, that they do often equalize, some-times excel men, in what ever they attempt; what reason can be given why they should not be improved? . . . Learning perfects and adorns the Soul, which all Creatures aim at. Nay more, a principal part of God's Image in Man's first Creation, consisted in Knowledge. Sin has clouded this: why should we not by instruction endeavour to repair that which shall be perfected in Heaven?[4]

In many ways, literary humanism should remain an ideal for our modern universities. We need to hear and understand people in the languages they themselves speak, for every language contains irreducible subtleties of meaning. And, of course, the independence of thought enabled by firsthand engagement of the sources is no respecter of gender.

In philosophy narrowly defined, scholasticism and Aristotle remained unchallenged until the scientific revolution. Aristotelian

---

4. Bathsua Makin, *An Essay to Revive the Antient Education of Gentlewomen in Religion, Manners, Arts & Tongues* (London, 1673), as quoted in Holly Faith Nelson, "Nascent Christian Feminism in Medieval and Early-Modern Britain," in *Being Feminist, Being Christian: Essays from Academia*, ed. Allyson Jule and Bettinga Tate Pedersen (New York: Palgrave MacMillan, 2006), 168–69. Our thanks to Holly Nelson for supplying us with this reference.

thinking provided the guidelines for rigorous inquiry in pursuit of metaphysical certitude.[5] Literary humanism proffered a practical attitude concerning the ultimate end of learning. For literary humanists, what mattered was preparation for participation in political life, a life of prudential engagement. The goal of education was to understand our aspirations and emotions and to discipline them in order to achieve a stance of cultured tolerance toward every member of society. This is why literary humanists were so preoccupied with language. For them, language, complex enough to express our most subtle reflections, set human beings apart from animals. Education had first to deal with language and meaning, for in all speech, words and sense are inseparably connected like body and soul. Literary humanists were convinced that we could best learn to live together by reading the experiences of others.

For them, liberal arts education gave one the ability to make decisions in the course of daily life that were based on moral virtues that one could not necessarily discover in nature. They believed not only that moral virtues escaped the scrutiny of inquiry into the natural world but also that scientific discoveries would always change, whereas the one constant in history was human existence and eternal questions concerning purpose, justice, wisdom, and happiness. These questions could not be answered by logic or scientific observation, which Aristotle's method appeared to favor.

Although literary humanists dismissed Aristotle's method of inquiry, they did not turn away from him altogether. They simply valued certain aspects of his philosophy more than others. Literary humanists particularly cherished Aristotle's notions of wisdom and virtue. Here they retained his emphasis on life in this world. Knowing what to do would depend a great deal on the circumstances in which one found oneself. At the same time, they thought that our reasons for how we acted depended very much on how we shaped our likes and dislikes. Reading texts in history, philosophy, and other disciplines could help the student to form moral character and develop a basis for sober judgment. Therefore they favored Aristotle's *Ethics* over any of his other works. → so does Baylor....

5. Nauert, *Humanism*, 15.

Literary Humanism and Christianity

When we examine literary humanism, we do not find a battle between intellectuals set to liberate the world from religious superstitions, on the one hand, and stubborn Christians standing against the progress of humanity by clinging to irrational conceptions of reality, on the other. Instead we see different attitudes among Christian thinkers. In fact, the most celebrated literary humanists, such as Erasmus of Rotterdam, Roger Asham, and the famous Hebrew scholar Johann Reuchlin, were Christians.

As Christians, they did not reject certain sources of knowledge because they deemed them unbiblical. This would be unreasonable for them, since, like Aquinas, they considered all intellectually and morally beneficial developments as gifts from God. Rather, they rejected certain ideas because these did not suit their definition of profitable knowledge. For example, although many of these literary humanists were Christians, they did not despise Aristotle because he was a pagan. In fact, it was the hallmark of Christian literary humanism to appreciate all truth as God's truth, whether it came from pagan or from Christian sources. Erasmus supplies a good example of their attitude when he writes, on reading the ancient pagan author Marcus Tullius Cicero, "I cannot read Tully *Of Old Age, Of Friendship*, his *Offices* or his *Tusculan Questions* without kissing the book, without a veneration for the soul of that divine heathen; and then, on the contrary, when I read some of our modern authors, their politics, economics and ethics—Good God, how jejune and cold they are."[6]

Erasmus shared with other humanists a notion of common grace, by which God in his providence had given much insight into human truths to pagan authors who anticipated the culmination and fullest explanation of what it means to be human in Christ as the ultimate divine source of truth. He was convinced that the academic disciplines were part of a divine plan to provide the church with the best of learning. Roger Asham, in his book on education entitled *The Schoolmaster*, similarly concluded that the writings of the most famous and eloquent ancient Greek authors are given to us by divine providence. Humanists such as these two offer us a

6. Erasmus, "The Pious Feast," in *English Humanism: Wyatt to Cowley*, ed. Joanna Martindale (Dover, NH: Croom Helm, 1985), 110.

fruitful model of learning: in the belief that reason is a divine gift given to all, we can celebrate truth wherever we find it.

Literary Humanists on Language

Because they viewed reason and affections as a unity, literary humanists insisted that language mattered. For them, rhetoric was not an unnecessary frill. Words carried real power because their effect on the emotions moved the mind and body to action. They did not believe that one could separate form (linguistic expression) from content (the message). Our modern notion to cut to the chase and present things in a frank, offhand manner without carefully chosen words—words often disparaged as frills and gimmicks or filled with the subtleties of inauthenticity—would sound very strange to them. In fact, for literary humanists, precision meant finding just the right word for the thing one wanted to express; the richness and complexity of human thought, affect, and ideas required a rich vocabulary rather than a trimmed-down version. Erasmus stressed our ability to use metaphors and other rhetorical devices to produce the most concrete picture possible of an idea.[7]

To summarize, literary humanists believed in the intimate and necessary connection between eloquence and wisdom, words and things. For them, poor writing evinced poor thinking; the decline of style inevitably would lead to the corruption of learning and life. They already understood the importance of language for our interpretation of the world, that experience and its linguistic expression are inseparable. As one literary humanist put it, speech is the gift by which we relate to one another. Language is grounded in experience, and experience can only be conveyed in language. We cannot separate meaning and truth from language. In the intimate connection between reason and language, between reason and thought, one finds the explanation for the literary humanist's disdain for scholastic terminology and technicalities of logic. According to literary humanism, the medieval system froze ideas and human experience into prefabricated molds and effectively killed learning by reducing it to memorizing and reiterating concepts.

7. Ibid., 38.

The whole reason for their emphasis on eloquence and rhetoric was to bring ideas to life through lively and suitable language.

I second!

Conclusion

Humanism in the early modern period was primarily a literary humanism, whose main goal was self-knowledge and character formation through the reading of edifying texts from the past. "Reading good books produces good people" could summarize its outlook. As Christians, we may have some doubts about the ability to defeat sin simply by reading edifying books, as if genuine conversion of one's moral values could take place without the intervention of God.

At the same time, however, we inherit from the literary humanists many good ideas about the value of literature and the arts. If you are a student and wonder why you should study literature, the old literary humanists would answer that by putting yourself in touch with some of the most excellent virtues and their pursuit by individuals in history, by viewing the depiction of vice and virtue in the literary and fine arts, and by studying philosophies that expand the horizon and help you to recognize and suppress your more selfish desires while encouraging behavior for the good of society, you will learn what it means to be human and become a wholesome influence in society. In addition, literary humanism urges us not to accept people's opinions about matters but to check out things for ourselves at their source, partially by reading texts in their original languages, settings, and contexts.

We should thus value literary humanism as a much-needed antidote to our current view of literature and the arts as subjective or as an unnecessary luxury for some elite, cultured people. Literary humanism also helps us remember that language is very powerful and that how we express ourselves reflects the content of what we say. Words are more than mere labels. Incidentally, it is instructive to apply this insight to the terminology we use to refer to the people who fill the lecture halls. As mentioned earlier, the Latin word from which the word "study" derives, *studium*, can also be rendered "desire," and so the student is one who desires to learn. Today we often refer to the student as a client or as the eventual "product" of an educational machinery. The mechanistic, business-like connotations of these terms tell us much about how our view of education has changed.

As university education moved out of its initial medieval milieu, it did not abandon its fundamental assumption that <u>learning was a deeply Christian activity</u>. Nor did it suffer from anxiety because the institution was in the world and relevant to this-worldly affairs. Rather, it heightened interest in the role and power of language, quite apart from Aristotelian categories that no longer seemed to do justice to all that was being learned.

At the same time, however, literary humanism offered a one-sided view of human reality, for it did not take science seriously enough. It focused too much on a merely mental-spiritual understanding of human nature, as if intellectual exercises would automatically transform people—a kind of mind-over-body philosophy. Unfortunately, it is not always the case that dwelling on beautiful and edifying things makes people more intelligent, let alone turn them into saints; in addition, contemplation of the beautiful in books often neglects the careful consideration of our everyday environment, of our bodies, and of nature. It is no surprise, then, that literary humanism evoked a backlash from science. Unfortunately, this reaction deepened a split between the arts and the sciences.

Study Questions

1. When you think of the Renaissance, do you think of humanism? Why or why not?
2. This chapter distinguishes between medieval humanism and literary humanism. Describe one good feature and one bad feature of literary humanism.
3. According to literary humanists, a liberal arts education could prepare one for participation in public life. Do you think this claim is still relevant?
4. Renaissance or literary humanism is often celebrated as freeing the human spirit from the shackles of religious belief. According to this chapter, is literary humanism necessarily antagonistic to Christianity?
5. Why is an emphasis on language important to any understanding of humanism?

4

SECULAR SCIENTIFIC
HUMANISM

This chapter recounts how science asserted itself against literary humanism and medieval scholasticism. It introduces Francis Bacon and René Descartes as key figures committed to emancipating truth from language and emotion. Their efforts instilled fresh confidence in reason as the final arbiter in intellectual matters, capable of delivering absolute certainty. Science eventually recombined with humanism in a very specific way to achieve a this-worldly, secular outlook we call secular scientific humanism. This chapter shows how Christians at that time continued to play a leading role in shaping university learning, especially the arts-sciences tension.

Introduction

Literary humanism had tried to free learning from Aristotelian scholasticism in order to obtain a less abstract model of education conducive to character formation and civic virtues. But even though in this endeavor literary humanism had built upon belief in the power of reason, a belief fostered by medieval humanism, it did not hold things together. Its eagerness to concentrate on literary sources and its willingness to leave science and metaphysics to Aristotelian categories eventually resulted in a correction. In its neglect of the sciences, literary humanism had already implied a split between moral truths found in the study of texts and in the study of nature. Unfortunately, the movement that now began to counter literary humanism's overemphasis on textual studies for the advancement of humankind drove a deeper wedge between the arts and the sciences by eventually entrenching a dualism in which the former, together with religion, became suspect as a merely subjective form of knowledge.

Like literary humanism, scientific secular humanism began by lashing out against Aristotelian scholasticism. We have already seen that Aristotle was attacked in the Renaissance by literary humanists for his stuffy, technical classifications. They did not think that his methodology was nimble enough for day-to-day application. By the seventeenth century Aristotelian scholasticism also came under attack from the rising new science:

> Aristotelian scholasticism was under pressure from four directions: its logic was attacked as over-complex and artificial; its rational theology as verbal sophisms not needed by the faithful and not cogent enough to convince the faithless; its physics as abstract and unempirical; its system of values as ascetically self-mutilating.[1]

Aristotelian argumentation suggested rhetorical excess; ideas such as fourfold causality were hopelessly outdated; and because scholasticism had taken over monastic education, Aristotelian virtues became associated with severe self-discipline. This Aristotle did not aid humanism, naturalism, or the advancement of learning.

With the rise of science, both Aristotle and literary humanism were attacked as "unscientific" by the champions of a neutral human rationality supposedly capable of cutting through all ambiguity caused by language, human emotions, and subjective imagination to a core of neutral, indisputable facts. This new enthusiasm for science, which purported to deal with the evident facts apart from any opinion, tradition, or convention, still shapes

---

1. Anthony Quinton, *Francis Bacon* (New York: Oxford University Press, 1980), 16.

our understanding of reason today. When one hears a skeptic oppose the uncertain impressions of moral or emotional ideas to the obvious facts of reason, one is encountering an understanding of truth that took shape in the seventeenth century.

What one expects from a university education has everything to do with one's ideas about what knowledge is, how it is obtained, and how it is passed on to others. This distinction between "what to" and "how to" becomes the main dividing line between the sciences' view of knowledge and the humanities' view of knowledge. This division is unfortunate, and the postmodern critique of science and humanism alike can help us overcome this science-versus-humanities divide to open up rich vistas of holistic and interdisciplinary possibilities.

The rise of modern science, including its effects on literary humanism, makes clear that intellectual history cannot be told primarily as a battle between either science and religion or the arts and religion. It is not a battle for truth in which unbiased scientific clarity distanced itself from Christianity. In fact, the greatest scientists of this period, to whom we owe revolutionary progress, such as Francis Bacon, Galileo, René Descartes, and Isaac Newton, to name only a few, were all Christians who saw no conflict whatsoever between their scientific endeavors and the Christian faith. Their Christian belief in the rational design of creation made possible the development of science in the first place.

But if the rise of science cannot be explained as a tug-of-war between science and religion, what did happen in the sixteenth and seventeenth centuries? This history should be understood as precipitating an enormous change in how people understood human rationality. When we want to map how we traveled from the Renaissance to the Enlightenment and to our own time, we need to examine the growing confidence in the ability of human reason *to see things as they really are, apart from metaphysical starting points or religious revelation.* Once we shift our attention to this phenomenon, we can see that both Christians and, much later, atheists participated in the same development.

The story of the rise of scientific reason turns on the separation of reason and language. If the importance of the connection between reason and language for literary humanists disrupted the unity of medieval humanism, the rise of scientific reason caused the wound to unity of knowledge to bleed anew. For science, language became merely a tool, not essential for understanding. Writing the history of the Royal Society, Thomas Sprat gloated already in the eighteenth century that science had nearly done away with metaphorical language to create a close correspondence between words and things.[2] The Royal Society's motto, moreover, was not to trust anyone's word.[3] In terms of rhetorical technique, this meant turning away from the humanistic injunction to prepare one's audience for one's message by establishing credibility and goodwill. The scientific facts alone mattered.

When one reads the story of science this way, it is possible to unite the most important subplots in the ascendancy of scientific reason, namely, empiricism and rationalism. Both concepts have the same goal: to free truth from the vagaries of language and emotion. Instead truth is to be founded on the absolute certainty of an unshakable foundation. This was to be the new method of the sciences. For Francis Bacon this foundation was empiricism, or the inductive method, by which one reasons from experiential data to higher conclusions. For the French thinker René Descartes, by contrast, the human mind was to provide the bedrock for truth. Both—one through empiricism, the other through rationalism—opposed language as suspect and contributed to a dualistic split between the arts and the sciences.

The following brief sections on these thinkers provide the context necessary to understand what comes to be the dominant view of reason and truth in the Enlightenment, the controlling belief of what education and the nature of the university ought to be, and the place of Christianity (or rather its irrelevance) in such a picture. Well-intentioned Christian scientists would contribute to their religion's intellectual marginalization.

Empiricism

At the beginning of *The Advancement of Learning*, Francis Bacon (1561–1626), writing in 1605, took stock of the main intellectual currents of his time. Bacon was to become a famous pioneer of the empirical (or inductive) method, and he explained

---

2. Thomas Sprat, *History of the Royal Society* (1667), ed. Jackson I. Cope and Harold Whitmore Jones (St. Louis: Washington University Press, 1958), 2.20.
3. Sprat, *History of the Royal Society*, facing the title page.

the unsatisfactory nature of the contemporary options. His first target was Aristotelian scholasticism, which he called disputatious learning; his second was the delicate learning of literary humanism.[4]

Although Bacon appreciated Aristotle's emphasis on observation, he rejected the medieval spin put on the Greek philosopher's writings and considered Aristotle's metaphysical categories in need of revision. According to Bacon, the main fault of the scholastics was their lack of genuine experimentation. Instead of working on the actual "stuff" of nature in contemplating God's creation, the scholastics slavishly followed Aristotle's books and merely elaborated on his observations. According to Bacon, they satisfied themselves with mental gymnastics so that the mind, working "upon itself, as the spider works his web," became endlessly engaged in idle speculation and brought forth "cobwebs of learning, admirable for the fineness of thread and work but of no substance or profit."[5]

Literary humanism fared little better than medieval humanism. For Bacon, literary humanism was marked by "the admiration of ancient authors, the hate of the schoolmen, the exact study of language, and the efficacy of preaching." Yet literary humanism was unscientific and misguided because it gave too much credence to language. Though not opposed to eloquence, Bacon feared the danger of an excessive infatuation with language. Literary humanists, he claimed, "hunt more after words than matter" and care more about "the sweet falling of the clauses, and the varying and illustration of their works with tropes and figures," than about "the weight of matter, worth of subject, soundness of argument, life of invention, or depth of judgment."[6]

Bacon considered the concerns of literary humanism frivolous; he opposed humanistic knowledge to knowledge that could reduce

4. A third, which need not concern us here, is what he calls the fantastic learning associated with the occult practices of magic, alchemy, and astrology.

5. Francis Bacon, "Of the Proficience and Advancement of Learning, Divine and Human," in *The Later Renaissance in England* (Boston: Houghton Mifflin, 1975), 403. Recent work on the history of science has shown that Bacon's view of medieval science was exaggerated and one-sided. For a general introduction to this history, see David C. Lindberg and Ronald L. Numbers, eds., *God and Nature: Historical Essays on the Encounter between Christianity and Science* (Berkeley: University of California Press, 1986).

6. Bacon, "Of the Proficience," 402.

human suffering and discomfort. For him, Renaissance humanists valued style over substance; when this humanism was taken to an extreme, they wanted to celebrate human potentiality almost as a self-contained *idea* in which usefulness played no part. Bacon would undoubtedly roll over in his grave if he knew of our modern-day preoccupation with self-fashioning and spin doctoring.

Bacon did not completely give up on humanism, however. In *The Advancement of Learning*, he acknowledged a role for humanist preoccupation with rhetoric. He saw the need for an alliance between reason and the imagination to enable the will to overcome the affections. Rhetoric could stir the imagination. In some ways, he merely wanted to correct an underappreciation of the place of scientific learning. Still, he did not share literary humanists' conviction of the necessary connection between form and content, between knowledge and language. He did not question the dualism of words and matter but rather entrenched it, reducing words to the status of mere "images" of matter.

Bacon made an enormous threefold contribution to the understanding of modern scientific method: objectivity, public knowledge, and progress. He emphasized the need to begin with unbiased observations of nature and to accumulate knowledge in this way. The scientific method does not depend merely on observation, however. Some postmodern attacks on objectivity suggest that science rests on this tenet alone. For Bacon, the accumulation of knowledge depended crucially on the ability of someone else to verify a claim about nature. In this way, he contributed to the growing emphasis on *public* knowledge. Under the aegis of science, knowledge that is valued is knowledge to which all have free and equal access; such knowledge can be demonstrated right before your eyes. Finally, he also helped promote the modern idea of progress based on ever-increasing knowledge.

Because of his contribution to scientific method, on the one hand, and his disdain for scholasticism and literary humanism, on the other, one can see how Bacon's work suggested a clean break with the past. He introduced a new method of discovering truth, the inductive method, which painstakingly gathers all available empirical evidence before drawing general conclusions. Bacon described the difference of his new method from Aristotelian science as the "true" scientific method that yields absolutely certain results:

There are and can exist but two ways of investigating and discovering truth. The one hurries on rapidly from the senses and particulars to the most general axioms, and from them, as principles and their supposed indisputable truth, derives and discovers the intermediate axioms. This is the way now in use. The other constructs its axioms from the senses and particulars, by ascending continually and gradually, till it finally arrives at the most general axioms, which is the true but unattempted way.[7]

Bacon believed that only with this new method could the sciences "establish a new and certain course for the mind from the first actual perceptions from the senses themselves."[8] Only the "formation of notions and axioms on the foundation of true induction"[9] could restore truth to absolute clarity. Bacon's inductive method, however, had a rival in this enterprise for certain knowledge. A second influential voice has shaped our conception of reason as *scientific* reason: working with the no-nonsense, no-frills, straight-up goods of facts. Like Bacon, René Descartes wanted to place knowledge on a firm footing. Unlike Bacon, however, Descartes began not with experience but with the mind. Whereas Bacon's approach has been called inductive reasoning, Descartes suggested deductive reasoning, the drawing of inferences from unshakable truths established by thought alone.

Rationalism

Like Bacon, René Descartes (1596–1650) pursued the goal of circumventing the idea of the mediation of truth by experience and language. Both wanted to fast-track reason by a clearer and more direct connection with reality. Neither of these thinkers ever dreamed of undermining Christianity with their methods. The general direction of their intention, however, was the opposite of the Christian idea that knowledge always involves trust in something greater than ourselves. Bacon and Descartes sought to place

7. Francis Bacon, *Novum Organum: Aphorisms Concerning the Interpretation of Nature and the Kingdom of Man* (1620) 1.19, in *Great Books of the Western World*, 54 vols. (Toronto: Encyclopaedia Britannica, 1952), 30:108.
    8. Ibid., 105.
    9. Ibid., 109.

trust in human reason itself to establish the reliability and hence the autonomy of the human mind.

Bacon sought clarity in the direct and indubitable evidence of experience, sifted through the critical faculty of reason, from which we then build more universal conclusions. Descartes, by contrast, consciously distanced himself from the senses because he felt strongly that the senses can always deceive. He started with the mental operation of doubt. For him, the one thing that is true beyond doubt is the fact that "I am doubting." Even in the worst-case scenario that God might be a deceiver, God could not meddle with the fact that I am doubting and hence thinking:

> Although it is not readily apparent that this doubt is useful, still it is the more so in that it frees us of all prejudices and paves an easy path for leading the mind away from the senses. Finally it makes it impossible for us to doubt further those things that we shall discover to be true.[10]

In a fateful step, Descartes defined the human being as "a thing that thinks."[11] In his quest for certainty, Descartes made emotions, language, and external reality separate from thought. Reason was now defined as thought without connection to the world of the senses. The mind became the core of the human being. From this basis, Descartes began to reconstruct all of reality, but all his deliberations remain haunted by the specter of a split between the body and the mind, between the world of the senses and the world of reason.

Descartes, like Bacon, hoped that his new philosophy would replace the teachings of Aristotle and give fresh impetus to the scientific interpretation of all reality. Science would in turn forever ban the uncertainty of emotions, subjective opinion, and religious beliefs. Scientific reason was constructed in response to the disillusionment with religion experienced by previous generations on account of the religious wars that had devastated much of Europe. One need only read the opening pages of his *Meditations* to sense Descartes's attitude of compassion and his desire to contribute to the betterment of society. Through scientific reason, he hoped

10. René Descartes, *Meditations on First Philosophy* (1641), trans. Donald A. Cress (Indianapolis: Hackett, 1979), 8.
11. Ibid., 19.

to go beyond the differences of subjective opinion by founding true knowledge on the model of self-evident truths. This model, which came to dominate the seventeenth century and still exerts its influence today, tended to reduce knowledge to what could be quantified, and considered as real what followed the model of mathematical and geometrical certainty. As Descartes put it, "Whether I be awake or asleep, two plus three makes five, and a square does not have more than four sides; nor does it seem possible that such obvious truths can fall under the suspicion of fallacy."[12]

In their different ways, Descartes and Bacon sought to remove obstacles to clear, rational thinking. The intellectual historian Isaiah Berlin has well described this attitude of scientific reasoning:

> The general, if not universal, tendency of the new philosophy was to declare that if the human mind can be cleared of dogma, prejudice and cant, of the organized obscurities and Aristotelian patter of the [medieval] schoolmen, then nature will at last be seen in the full symmetry and harmony of its elements, which can be described, analysed and represented by a logically appropriate language—the language of the mathematical and physical sciences.[13]

The new philosophy was meant to liberate humanity; scientific reason sprang from humanitarian motives. Both Bacon and Descartes were very much committed to enhancing human welfare and promoting better life on earth. The ticket to this was to make humans more rational and therefore wiser, more just, virtuous, and happy. In this way, then, the rise of science is also a kind of humanism: secular scientific humanism. Reason, freed from the trammels of tradition, history, and language, would discover the true ends of human existence. Reason, unfettered by any other authority than its own, would inevitably discover what is best for mankind.

Secular Scientific Humanism

One can see the mutual reintegration of humanism and science in the thought of the political philosopher Thomas Hobbes

12. Ibid., 15.
13. Isaiah Berlin, *The Proper Study of Mankind: An Anthology of Essays*, ed. Henry Hardy and Roger Hausheer (London: Pimlico, 1998), 330.

(1588–1679). Like Bacon and Descartes, Hobbes believed in the triumph of the scientific method and became famous for applying this method to the most intractable of all human activities, politics. But he also incorporated rhetoric, as emphasized by literary humanists and respected by Bacon. Hobbes thus represents an attempt to heal the breach between the arts and the sciences. This reconciliation, however, happened under the aegis of scientific reason, and although it included the use of rhetoric, there was no sense of the embeddedness of truth in language. Furthermore—and connected with this limitation—Hobbes's intervention left little room for religious faith in the achievement of genuine knowledge. He helped put modern scientific humanism on a thoroughly secular footing; humanism after him had little to do with a religious desire to be incarnational in the world and everything to do with leaving theology in the intellectual dust.

Hobbes's philosophical system took shape in the crucible of tensions between the claims of science and humanism.[14] His education had been thoroughly humanistic, dominated by the study of rhetoric and a vision of civic man inspired by ancient Roman rhetorical treatises. This education prepared him for the role of personal tutor and secretary in several households of the gentry and nobility. In his forties, however, Hobbes abandoned the ideals of humanism and expressed a distaste for rhetoric in favor of a more purely scientific outlook. He went on to apply this technique to the study of politics, a radical innovation that made him famous.

Hobbes found very attractive the concerns and methods of science. He read Euclid and began to participate in scientific studies, even conducting his own optical experiments. At the same time, he revised his views on the value of rhetoric. One indicator of this change can be found in his treatment of Aristotle's *Art of Rhetoric*.[15] Like his book on ethics, the *Art of Rhetoric* was one of only a few of Aristotle's books to continue to have influence on the literary humanists. Hobbes's interest in this Aristotelian

14. We gratefully acknowledge our indebtedness to the work of the renowned historian of ideas Quentin Skinner, who has traced the development of Hobbes to argue for his unique blending of science and humanism, for this section. Quentin Skinner, *Reason and Rhetoric in the Philosophy of Hobbes* (New York: Cambridge University Press, 1996), 258.

15. Skinner, *Reason and Rhetoric*, 256–57.

work should have been a sign of his literary humanism. But in his translation of the *Art of Rhetoric*, Hobbes blatantly altered some of Aristotle's statements to suggest that rhetoric was self-serving and not interested in truth. He was turning away even from this vestige of humanism. In an early work on government, Hobbes insisted that resistance against rhetorical technique should characterize not only the natural sciences but also the moral sciences.

The humanist rhetoricians endorsed an understanding of wisdom based on past experience, a practical form of wisdom Aristotle called prudence. Hobbes, too, believed in wisdom, but he took care to distinguish prudence from wisdom based on the knowledge of propositions and the correct naming of things, which was wisdom proper. Christian humanists in both the medieval and the early modern periods had maintained a sense of the messiness of our being in the world, the relatedness between thinking and acting, and the role of language in shaping both. Hobbes contributed to our modern, and rather reductive, view of language as merely a tool for expressing ideas. He attempted to establish a more direct relationship between words and things because, for him, wisdom lay in a mathematical understanding of propositions and their logical unfolding.

Besides literary humanism's view of language, Hobbes also attacked its ideal of civic man. The literary humanists saw the exercise of the duties of citizenship as the goal of human formation and took a dim view of scholarly and contemplative life. (One can see here the beginnings of dualism and their disdain for aspects of medieval humanism.) Hobbes, by contrast, considered involvement in public life meddlesome, inspired by self-interest. He considered the duties of citizenship to be best exercised in scientific study, arguing that we owe the advance of civilization to nothing other than scientific efforts and discoveries. Hobbes's emphasis on the scholarly and contemplative life, an essentially private life, can be reconciled with Bacon's insistence on knowledge that is publicly verifiable. Both distanced themselves from rhetoric and the humanist belief in dialogue and compromise as driven by inexactitude and ultimately by self-interest.

With the writing of his major work, *Leviathan*, Hobbes reincorporated some basic humanist assumptions. He came to the view that reason alone would not induce people to change their thinking, that instead they needed to be cajoled by the moving force of eloquence.[16] Hobbes did not betray a crisis of confidence in rationality or a sense of the deep embeddedness of truth in language, such as we find in our contemporary postmodern situation. He did, however, express the view that reason does not have the power on its own to convince people to act. It is not as powerful as self-interest. People will dispute reason and the clear proofs of science if these appear to jeopardize their personal interests. So he fought fire with fire. He appeared willing to concede that rhetoricians could be interested in truth, not just verbal gymnastics, if the claims of science (which he held to be true) could be promoted by the use of rhetoric. In other words, truth-oriented scientists could use rhetoric safely.

The rhetorical achievement of *Leviathan* set a precedent for the future of philosophy, at least English philosophy. It is a precedent pertinent to our discussion of the relationship between skepticism and belief:

> In teaching philosophy to speak English, Hobbes at the same time taught it a particular tone of voice. As we have seen, the tone is very much that of the sane and moderate *savant* beset on all sides by fanaticism and stupidity. We cannot expect reason to triumph, the tone implies, since the foolish and ignorant will always be in a majority. But we can at least hope to discomfit them by wielding the weapons of ridicule, deriding their excesses, sneering at their errors, drawing our readers into a scornful alliance against their general benightedness.[17]

Hobbes made scientific reason persuasive where it had not been completely so on its own. He enlisted the humanist appreciation of rhetoric, though without reviving the humanist ideals of negotiation and the civic man. Hobbes combined science and rhetoric to achieve a secular scientific humanism.

OK, I think Hobbes is boring.

Conclusion

Humanism turned a corner with Bacon, Descartes, and Hobbes: scientific reasoning had come of age. Science may not yet have won

16. Ibid., 426.
17. Ibid., 436.

a conclusive victory and the totality of its truth value may not yet have been evident to all, but the rational and scientific community of the seventeenth century found in people's self-interest a ready explanation for this failure. Furthermore, humanist rhetoric had been enlisted in the service of science's advancement, although it was really a marriage of convenience.

It would not be long before the objectivist view of truth propagated by secular scientific humanism won out and education became equated with the compilation of facts. Writing in the nineteenth century, Charles Dickens caricatured this development in *Hard Times*. In the novel's opening episode, the teacher Mr. Gradgrind drills into his students (with the best of intentions, of course) that "facts alone are wanted in life. Plant nothing else, root out everything else. You can only form the minds of reasoning animals upon Facts; nothing else will ever be of service to them. This is the principle on which I bring up my own children, and this is the principle on which I bring up these children. Stick to the facts, sir."[18] We can see in Dickens's parody that any aspiration toward holism in education had fallen upon hard times indeed. Language had become instrumental, divorced from reason and degraded as its handmaid.

Based on the teachings of Bacon and Descartes, a view of science had emerged in which facts were directly accessible to anyone who would open their eyes and exercise their reason. Hobbes had taught that the role of language was merely as an instrument in conveying these facts. The crucial underlying assumption was that every human being could share in a common pool of knowledge accessed by reason. If people would think and experiment long enough, the same lights would go on for everyone and all would agree on the facts.

The question that emerges for the Christian student is whether reason, with or without rhetoric, vanquished Christianity, consigning it to the intellectual rubbish heap of what Quentin Skinner calls "general benightedness." The second half of this book will address this question with reference to subsequent historical developments and Christian and non-Christian responses to secular scientific humanism. But first, we want to summarize the strengths

18. Charles Dickens, *Hard Times* (1854) (Oxford: Oxford University Press, 1991), 1.

and weaknesses of scientific humanism in the time period with which it is most readily associated, the Enlightenment. In exposing dualism as the main problem of Enlightenment thinking, we will focus on the split between faith and reason that the Enlightenment handed down to us.

Study Questions

1. In your opinion, are science and humanism compatible?
2. What are the differences between secular scientific humanism and the other humanisms described so far?
3. In what fundamental regard are Bacon and Descartes alike?
4. According to Quentin Skinner, how does Hobbes blend scientific principles with humanistic ones? What, then, is secular scientific humanism, and what kind of voice does it exhibit?

5

DARE TO THINK!

Enlightenment Humanism and Dualism

THIS CHAPTER SUMMARIZES HOW, WITH the Enlightenment, dualism became the reigning mode for experiencing reality. It defines dualism and argues that its divides go hand in hand with the tacit acceptance of human reason as the universally valid arbiter of truth. The chapter invites the reader to appreciate the benefits of the Enlightenment and to recognize its limitations. It is a transitional chapter anticipating our description of the necessary and multifaceted critique of the Enlightenment project, an assessment which has contributed to the widespread impression that the contemporary university is in a state of disarray.

Introduction

By the middle of the seventeenth century, science was in the ascendant. It concentrated people's attention on the disciplined, organized, publicly shared study of this world. Scientific principles had also exerted a strong influence on the study of such subjects as political theory and philosophy. Although science had called the tune, it had achieved a reconciliation with humanism. Thomas Hobbes's intellectual journey provides one prominent example of the marriage of scientific and rhetorical (or humanistic) traditions.[1] The humanism that emerged from this fusion initially made room for Christian belief; ultimately it was indebted to the Christian heritage of the West for explanations as to why humans mattered. Hobbes himself may have been a Christian of sorts, but perhaps not. Even if his intention was somehow to purify thought and rid Christianity of overzealous enthusiasts, the program of thought he promoted developed into an intellectual path that led many thinkers away from Christianity altogether.

In the seventeenth and eighteenth centuries, the loss of belief was not considered inevitable or even desirable by many other intellectuals. They generally sought to preserve a place for God while allowing men and women to get on with close scrutiny of the natural world. But as phenomena that had formerly been attributed to God's mysterious workings were claimed by science to be nothing but rule-governed natural processes, more and more people separated science and religion into two realms. They venerated God as the Maker who then left his creation to run on the principles he had built into it.

The picture of God as a watchmaker, and the world as his watch, became a favorite metaphor for the relationship between God and world and by implication between religion and science. Timepieces had by the eighteenth century become exquisite items of engineering; they attested the human power to create something intricate, delicate, beautiful, and useful. A perfectly made watch would never break down, never need rewinding. The watch symbolized many of the most important values of the Enlightenment: order, industry, and the ability of humans to govern their environment.[2] To call God a watchmaker was high praise indeed.

1. There are other equally interesting stories, some just as prominent, and certainly not all English. Michel de Montaigne's skepticism profoundly influenced not only Bacon but the wider development of philosophical thought, and he injected into it rhetorical innovation through his commitment to the essay form. Hobbes was himself influenced by the French during his exile, after which he again embraced the rhetorical tradition. Voltaire, who lived a century later, remains a byword for French and Enlightenment rationality. One could list numerous other thinkers, particularly in Western Europe.

2. Dava Sobel, *Longitude: The True Story of a Lone Genius Who Solved the Greatest Scientific Problem of His Time* (New York: Walker, 1995), a historical story

Yet even if God was being praised for being Supreme Reason or the Great Watchmaker and even if people imagined themselves to be imitating God in their pursuit of reason, industry, and order, God was being put to one side. A great chasm opened up between the realm of the Creator and the created order. God was no longer seen to be actively involved in sustaining his creation. Rather, nature ticked along on its own like a well-designed clock. This dualistic view of God and creation was also applied to the human mind. Reason, like the world, had become self-sufficient and could now arrive at even the highest truths without any assistance from God.

The previous chapter examined how both Bacon and Descartes drew on reason as the judge of truth, although they did so from two different starting points. Bacon was more empirical in his approach, moving from the exact observation of nature to general principles. Descartes, by contrast, was rationalistic in making the mind the measure of truth. Their approaches had in common a trust in human reason, as opposed to faith, tradition, and authority. This trust in reason as a reliable guide into all truth united both empiricists and rationalists under the banner of the Enlightenment with its enthusiasm for independent thought. Hardly anyone has exemplified the spirit of the Enlightenment better than the German philosopher Immanuel Kant.

Sapere aude!

Immanuel Kant (1724–1804) lived in the Prussian city of Königsberg, where he spent his entire life, eventually teaching and writing as a philosophy professor at the university. In 1784 he wrote a short and very famous essay with the title "An Answer to the Question: What Is Enlightenment?"[3] In this essay, Kant described enlightenment as "man's emergence from his self-incurred immaturity."[4] In using the term "immaturity," Kant drew

---

made into a television drama, captures exquisitely the fascination with time and its practical usefulness in eighteenth-century England.

3. Immanuel Kant, "An Answer to the Question: What Is Enlightenment?" in *From Modernism to Postmodernism: An Anthology*, ed. Lawrence Cahoone (Cambridge, MA: Blackwell, 1996), 51–57.

4. Ibid., 51.

on and confirmed a crucial metaphor of Enlightenment thought, that of human progress as the process of maturing from infancy to adulthood:

> *Immaturity* is the inability to use one's own understanding without the guidance of another. This immaturity is *self-incurred* if its cause is not lack of understanding, but lack of resolution and courage to use it without the guidance of another. The motto of enlightenment is therefore: "*Sapere aude!*" Have courage to use your *own* understanding.[5]

Kant here summed up the basic attitude of the Enlightenment, which ushered in a period also known as modernity. We saw this metaphor deployed in the article giving advice to atheists discussed at the start of the Preface.

For Kant, as for most other Enlightenment thinkers, tradition and authority meant the church and theology. Like many others, he was tired of the church in all its quarreling manifestations and desired a better society based on universal rational insights. Simply put, neither God nor the church but enlightened reason would assure a better society. This does not mean, however, that Kant was uninterested in theology or that he wanted to jettison morality. But he argued for a "pure faith" of moral religion that would be independent of the church and religious factions, whose divisiveness could never guarantee social improvement. Kant believed that "in matters which ought to be moral and soul improving by nature, reason has wrest itself free from the burden of faith constantly exposed to the arbitrariness of its interpreters."[6]

Kant's faith was a faith in the moral ability of humankind to improve itself by adhering to maxims that were universally recognized. These moral imperatives could not be derived from empirical observation (science) or from religious practice. That the Ten Commandments, for example, contained many such rules was only incidental; they merely showed that the biblical religion was an advancement on other pagan faiths, but they themselves only expressed in mythological terms the moral laws we can expound

---

5. Ibid. (emphasis original).
6. Immanuel Kant, "Religion within the Boundaries of Mere Reason" (1793), trans. George di Giovanni, in *Religion and Rational Theology* (New York: Cambridge University Press, 1996), 159.

through human reason. Religion is merely a private expression of these truths, one form of "the gospel of the realm of reason."[7]

Dualism as Worldview   ↗ *important*

With this teaching, Kant and the Enlightenment put in place a structural split. Reason was radically separated from faith, freedom from authority. This split can go by many names, of which the most common is dualism, in which one divides the universe into opposing parts or aspects. Other forms of dualism followed, all of which found a home in university thinking: matter versus spirit; naturalism versus supernaturalism; reason versus emotion; mind versus body; sight versus touch; science versus the arts.

To give just one example of dualism, in the eighteenth century many people (mostly men) associated scientific rationality with male prowess and the comforts of religion with female weakness. From this pairing stemmed an unfortunate association of an appreciation of literature and the arts with females, figured as emotional, and the privileging of business and the hard sciences as more masculine and worthwhile activities. This prejudice lingers. In our teaching experience, students often hate to take compulsory first-year English courses; many, mostly males, will freely confess to considering such courses as irrelevant to the "real world"; some express disdain for poetry, which they consider to be emotional and "for girls." Such separations betray an attitude owing to Enlightenment principles.

As Enlightenment attitudes took hold, many Christians accepted the split and entrenched it by arguing for a strictly rational Christianity.[8] For some, this split allowed them to reinforce certain gendered structures of authority. Others appealed to reason as justification for dismantling Christianity's claim to the truth of certain tenets of belief as historical events, such as the resurrection. It did not matter whether the resurrection actually happened, they argued; it only mattered that the resurrection was part of the story

7. Immanuel Kant, "The Conflict of the Faculties" (1798), ibid., 284.
8. So, e.g., the German thinker G. E. Lessing, who wanted to protect the Christian faith by removing it from the contingencies of history. Or the famous New Testament scholar Rudolf Bultmann, whose demythologization of the New Testament advocated the same basic move.

that one accepted on faith. People who adopted this strategy had accepted Descartes's deep and enduring distrust of history, which he passed on to all those who follow in his footsteps. The Baconian empiricist, by contrast, held that miracles simply do not happen; after all, everyday experience tells us so. Many Christians not only allowed Descartes and Bacon to call the tune; they also agreed that whatever truths one did accept had to be held as personal convictions only. It did not matter whether or not they were historical and publicly acknowledgable truths as long as one believed them, as long as they were true for oneself. Such Christians accepted a dualistic split between public and private realms. One often hears similar subjectivist opinions among today's Christians. Statements such as "I don't believe in doctrine but I believe in Jesus" or "The church doesn't matter; what matters are Christians" arise from the same dualisms as the Enlightenment, where personal conviction is opposed to doctrine, tradition, and institutions.

Although these assertions may issue from a deep desire for authentic piety, they nonetheless incarnate the Enlightenment spirit, cloaked in Christian lingo. The confessional stance that pits truehearted belief against the institutionalized church and doctrine is in essence indebted to the best Enlightenment philosophy. It simply reiterates Kant's antiauthoritarian attitude by defining itself against tradition. This form of Christian dualism is ironic because those who hold such pious views often defend truehearted belief against overintellectualization. Contrary to their intentions, however, the refusal to recognize that even our most heartfelt feelings are worldview-dependent does more damage than good. By retreating into the pure experience of faith, Christians have not, in fact, managed to separate spirituality from thought and worldview; rather, they have uncritically accepted certain modernist assumptions about thinking.

For Protestants, there is another subtle but cutting irony: one of our most cherished metaphors, that of the lone Protestant soldier standing on the pages of the Bible alone to battle tradition and all its evils falls into the same trap as Kant's divinization of reason. Cut off from tradition, faith becomes completely subjective. This ahistorical, nonincarnational interpretive approach, rooted in a specific historical development, is blind and subjectivist. When it comes to combating dualism, the church has often failed to respond adequately to the challenge of scientific secular humanism.

Christianity's Response to Secular Scientific Humanism

By the middle of the nineteenth century, the Christian church had come to see itself as besieged by a humanism apparently incompatible with a supernaturalism required by orthodox belief. It responded in two distinct ways. A social gospel attempted to accommodate a scientific worldview by minimizing the supernatural elements within Christianity and emphasizing its essentially humanitarian character, which it shared with other world religions and with secular humanism. In the twentieth century, emphasis on the social gospel left Christianity open to secularizing cultural developments that were inherently destabilizing because they rendered meaningless the very religious assumptions upon which the gospel of "Christian" humanitarianism operated. One of the most popular religious books of the 1960s was a confessional work entitled *Honest to God*, in which a theologian voiced his serious doubts about his faith, at least as traditionally understood.[9] It was good to be honest, bold, and to distance oneself from tradition.

A second trajectory arose out of parts of the church that insisted on Christianity's supernatural elements but otherwise accepted a scientific model of truth. These dualistic Christians emphasized one's personal relationship with God; religion became ever more private. Forms of Christianity committed to defending its supernatural aspects reacted against the Enlightenment by emphasizing a personal commitment to a set of beliefs and developing an adversarial posture against prevailing cultural developments. In so doing, this branch of Christianity became increasingly concerned with "fundamentals" and rigid about what constituted Christian belief. This branch reinforced a basic split between religious faith (as subjective piety) and scientific reason (as objective, publicly shared facts).[10]

9. John A. T. Robinson, *Honest to God* (Philadelphia: Westminster, 1963). In the 1960s there was, to be sure, a flourishing tradition of humanism that gladly embraced the death of God and wanted to see the human as simply and purely a product of the natural world. One problem for this tradition was that it seemed dependent on an entirely mechanistic understanding of the world. In this picture humans could be justified only in the most minimal terms—e.g., the principle of noncruelty or a calculation of what might be most good for the greatest number of people.

10. This development may seem odd, for a rigid belief in fundamentals would appear to go hand in hand with the facts of scientific, mechanistic thinking—and so it does. But the increasing emphasis in the broader culture on nature's ability to supply

Undeniably, each of these reactions preserves important elements of Christian orthodoxy. The social gospel upholds the church's mandate to live the life of the new age, testifying to redeemed humanity and creation by social action. Evangelical fundamentalism retains the church's emphasis on evangelization and Spirit-filled, vibrant, and relational Christianity. But both are incomplete halves of the full gospel. In the end, the humanistic social gospel and fundamentalism would both be caught off guard by the collapse of Enlightenment ideals from the 1960s onward, the one by finding itself bereft of its old intellectual buddies, the other by celebrating a victory it had not really won in a game it really should not have been playing.

Advances of Enlightenment Humanism

The Enlightenment wasn't all bad. In the era leading up to it, religion dominated. Many people, however, were increasingly disenchanted by what they saw as the senseless bickering between the two dominant forms of Christianity in Europe, Catholicism and Protestantism. Such religious infighting often escalated into violence and all-out war. There were also famous examples of opposition on religious grounds to scientific discoveries and daring ideas such as Galileo's. Religion often appeared to resist new ideas, exemplifying an attitude opposite of "dare to think!" And there was still the problem of popular belief in magic, alchemy, and astrology. For all these reasons, *Sapere aude!* heralded a fresh intellectual breeze.

In virtually any field of endeavor imaginable, one can find revolutionary advances in thought and culture that date from the Enlightenment. The scientific revolution directly contributed to the development of Enlightenment principles. It produced classical Newtonian physics, the discovery of the circulation of the blood, the foundations of modern chemistry, and countless other fundamental breakthroughs that have enabled the development of modern technologies. The Industrial Revolution resulted from the many practical discoveries and applications made in this era,

---

all the answers led to an emphasis by some Christians on supernatural aspects of belief and one's personal subscription to these beliefs, and this emphasis in turn encouraged subjective and private religion.

chronicled in such novels as George Eliot's *Adam Bede,* set in 1799. The rustic hero of this novel speaks with great confidence in modern developments: "there's such a thing as being over-speritial; we must have something beside the Gospel i' this world. Look at the canals, an' th' aqueducs, an' th' coal-pit engines, and Arkwright's mills there at Cromford; a man must learn summat beside Gospel to make them things, I reckon."[11] While Eliot was not suggesting that the Bible or Christianity be set aside, she was questioning an otherworldly separation betweeen spirituality and practical advances in this world through human know-how. This period also saw the founding of the social sciences and, in litera-ture, the growth of the realistic novel. In philosophy, stunning works of originality, complexity, and a this-worldly focus were being produced, of which Immanuel Kant's own writings stand as a major example.

Political and social revolutions took this line of thinking to perhaps its farthest extreme. The American Revolution of 1776 and the French Revolution of 1789 attested to the power of ques-tioning previously held assumptions of governance. The French Revolution sounded the defining optimistic theme of "Liberty, Equality, Fraternity!" Mary Wollestonecraft's essay on the rights of women in 1792, which one scholar has called "one of the most important documents in the history of feminist thought,"[12] helped pave the way for a revolution in social relations and identity.

George Eliot (the pen name of Mary Ann Evans) is among a select group of women who exemplify some of the most pro-found aspects of modernity. She does so through both her literary achievements and her life. Eliot challenged the assumptions of a male-dominated society, prevailing sexual ethics, and traditional ideas about the place of God in human society. To her, what really mattered was other human beings in all their otherness and variety. In her novels she stressed faithful description of nature carefully observed and a gentle acceptance of others, with all their foibles. We have already seen how she also recorded some of the great achievements resulting from intellectual advances. She was most harsh on characters who enforced strict religious systems

11. George Eliot, *Adam Bede* (1859), (New York: Penguin, 1980), 11.
12. Robert Demaria in Robert Demaria, ed., *British Literature, 1640–1789: An Anthology* (Cambridge, MA: Blackwell, 1996), 1185.

or subscribed to a narrow understanding of what people needed to know to flourish.

In the spirit of the Enlightenment, Eliot challenged not only traditional religious ethics but also the entire edifice of traditional Christianity. She could achieve prophetic stature in doing so. One of her contemporaries described an evening spent with her at the University of Cambridge:

> I remember how, at Cambridge, I walked with her once in the Fellows' Garden of Trinity, on an evening of rainy May; and she . . . taking as her text the three words . . . God, Immortality, Duty— pronounced, with terrible earnestness, how inconceivable was the first, how unbelievable the second, and yet how peremptory and absolute the third. . . . I listened, and night fell; her grave majestic countenance turned toward me like a sibyl's in the gloom.[13]

Here was a countenance for the intellectuals of the era. By the middle of the nineteenth century, Enlightenment rationality had made it possible—though still risky—to express disdain for belief in God and Immortality while elevating Duty toward others.

Significantly, in this recollection written in 1881, an ordinary human being is elevated to the level of prophet and sibyl. Certain ancient sibylline prophecies were read as foretelling that the final coming of Christ would be preceded by the reign of an emperor who ushered in a golden age. In this context, the golden age is connected not with the return of Christ but with enlightenment and the full flourishing of secular humanism. Religion is replaced by science and the arts, mysticism and spirituality by aesthetics. In this instance, a famous woman and literary figure fulfills the role of prophet. One of the challenges confronting Christian feminists and social theorists is to disentangle aspects of social reform from the turn away from Christian belief with which they coincide. Christian students must ask searching questions about the apparent complicity of traditional structures of belief with social practices we would not wish on anyone.

All of these advances derived from a fresh willingness on the part of an increasing number of people to concentrate on human affairs and the natural world. The light provided by the Enlighten-

---

13. F. W. H. Myers, quoted in Stephen Gill, "Introduction," George Eliot, *Adam Bede* (1859), (London: Penguin, 1985), xii.

ment truly dazzled people. It represented the culmination of slowly developing trends in Western intellectual culture, trends that, once put in place, seemed to lead inexorably to the freedom of human beings in a world previously dominated by the presence and authority of God and his select representatives in the Church.

Sapere aude! Dare to think! This motto should remain an enduring mark of the modern university. It represents an absolutely fundamental attitude toward learning in higher education. It's a very positive challenge, calling for an exhilarating attitude of risk-taking in the learner's inner being and holding out the promise of achievement.[14] We all acquire deeply held assumptions from our parents and the environment in which we grow up, and these assumptions need to be probed. At some point, we have to reconsider the ideas that have been implanted in us as facts we are not really invited to question. Until recently, the university was seen as the great adventure where one was pushed to think for oneself.

vouched

Conclusion

The freedom and courage to think for oneself are, of course, vitally important in university life, but they become rather dangerous when exercised on the conviction that, by definition, thinking needs to be completely separate from tradition and authority.[15] While we insist that critical thinking and the intelligent questioning of authority and tradition are essential elements in a university education, we believe that students should be aware of the risks and limitations of such an approach to the intellectual life in general and university education in particular.

Given free rein, this intoxicating passion for knowledge on the basis of human reason seems quite naïve. Who decides what is rational? For the Enlightenment thinkers (as for many today), this is a silly question; reason, they argue, is neutral and leads

14. For a compendium of the heroes from such a perspective, see Warren Allen Smith, *Who's Who in Hell: A Handbook and International Directory for Humanists, Freethinkers, Naturalists, Rationalists, and Non-theists* (New York: Barricade, 2000).

15. The early disillusionment of this principle came for Enlightenment enthusiasts with the French Revolution and its "Reign of Terror," which proved beyond doubt that universal reason may easily translate into arbitrary rule of those whose reason is more reasonable than others'.

us where it will. The postmodern reply is curt and to the point: people *use* reason. They use it to defend *their* freedom and justify *their* power. Much depends on this insight. Both Cartesian and Baconian rationalists failed to acknowledge that they defined in advance what counts as reasonable. Their interpretive prejudice, their worldview, prematurely determined the outcome.

Moreover, what is natural and reasonable often changes over time. In contrast to the eighteenth-century model of male rationality and stability versus female emotionality and fickleness, today some empiricists will speak of nature as the female Gaia in opposition to the idea of a God behind nature, whom they demonize as violent and male. In this case, Enlightenment dualism has been chastened by feminism. To take a different example, intellectuals in the eighteenth century often argued for a public social adherence to the tenets of reason and complained of a subversive reality in the lives of individuals, most often because of their class. More recently scholars have come to see such a view as giving prejudicial favor to the status quo; revisionist historiography has championed the rights of the underclass along lines less indebted to a certain abstract conception of rationality. Belief in reason can be detached from real life.

With the Enlightenment, at any rate, dualism itself emerged as the privileged worldview in the university setting. The departure from Aquinas is complete with the clear confrontation between Christian orthodox faith and secular philosophy. Kant himself, the great spokesperson of the Enlightenment, had simply no room for religious observances.[16] Reason—and thus rational religion—was by nature detached from communal practice and resided in the individual. Here indeed we find the secular humanism where the self is captain of its soul and where our humanity consists in self-mastery.

Yet above the dualistic conclusions of secular scientific humanism, one other prominent voice at this time is to be heard, arguing for a more Christian humanism. Our argument for the relevance of Christian thinking in and for the university as well as for our recovery of humanism as the goal of university experience can begin with Giambattista Vico (1668–1744), in some ways the

16. Manfred Kuehn, *Kant: A Biography* (New York: Cambridge University Press, 2001), 318.

founder of the modern human sciences and a precursor to radical changes in thought that would occur much later.

Study Questions

1. Immanuel Kant used the phrase *Sapere aude!* ("Dare to think!") against the church and religious traditions. Do you think Christians should accept the dare?
2. The authors define dualism in terms of a separation of faith and reason. What is deism? How does the picture of God as a watchmaker illustrate this problem?
3. What other manifestations of dualism do the authors suggest with reference to public life, the emotions, and the arts? Have you experienced any of these in your university education to date?
4. In light of the previous two questions, how do you, as a Christian, reconcile the interpretation of Scripture with the role of the church and tradition in interpretation? Can you see how the Protestant principle of *sola scriptura* could lead to interpretive dualism?
5. If the Enlightenment discourages the idea that religion is intrinsic to truth and thought, should Christians oppose the Enlightenment altogether?

6

THE BIRTH
OF THE HUMANITIES

Giambattista Vico's Critique of the Enlightenment

THIS CHAPTER ARGUES THAT THE humanities arose from a *Christian* critique of the Enlightenment's concept of reason and truth. Rather than confirming the general trend to apply the scientific method to the study of human culture, the Christian humanist Giambattista Vico insisted on the distinctiveness of humanistic studies, whose principal goal is self-knowledge rather than the functionally directed know-how of the natural sciences.

Although Enlightenment dualism was fast becoming the dominant outlook of European intellectuals, some questioned the application of scientific method to all areas of knowledge. Why should this one particular way of describing reason and truth dictate to all university disciplines what counts as reasonable and true knowledge? These were the questions raised by Giambattista Vico (1688–1744), professor of rhetoric and history at the University of Naples in Italy. By asking these questions, Vico distanced himself from the confidence that was swelling in the physical sciences. He serves as an example of someone who recognized the limits of secular scientific humanism long before postmodernism ever appeared on the horizon of intellectual history. He did so on Christian grounds, because of his belief in the image of God in humans.

Vico had initially been a fan of Descartes's writings, but in the middle of his career he suddenly turned to oppose Descartes's notion that human knowledge has to conform to the mathematical ideal of certainty, an expectation that had begun to dominate academic disciplines with the rise of science. Indeed, Descartes himself had already noticed this problem. Where in the study of history or art or literature can we find strict definitions, rigorous proofs established by repeated experiments with exactly the same outcome? Where in the critical analysis of human cultural expression do we find the absolute, timeless, self-evident truths Descartes was looking for as the bedrock on which to build by meticulous deduction the whole edifice of human knowledge? Just like Descartes, therefore, Vico understood that the application of this scientific method to human culture and history would not yield very much fruit. Vico, however, denied Descartes's conclusion that knowledge of history, art, and literature (in effect, knowledge derived from human culture) is therefore inferior. Instead Vico challenged Descartes's rationalistic premise. Vico, in other words, understood that Descartes's seeming fortress of foundational rational truths rested on a particular worldview.

Vico began his criticism of Descartes by challenging the latter's definition of true knowledge as mathematical certainty. Mathematics, Vico argued, appears noncontradictory and certain only because it is arbitrary. Unlike applied mathematics or empirical observation, mathematical theory is a self-enclosed system whose perfection is possible because humans invented it in the first place. The phenomena of nature, by contrast, are messy and tend to upset neat categorization. The problem with scientific knowledge, that is, knowledge of nature, is that it will always remain foreign to us, since we neither create nor absolutely control nature. Only God, who has created and sustains nature, has real "inside" knowledge of nature. What humans do produce (and hence are able to know with relative certainty), however, is culture.

Vico completed his argument against Descartes by suggesting another kind of knowledge. Against the illusion of perfect knowledge according to the mathematical model, and against empirical observation of nature, which remains foreign to us, Vico proposed the knowledge that would become the foundation of the human sciences: self-knowledge. This knowledge was different from knowledge based on religious faith, rationalist deduction, or scientific induction. Unlike faith-based or intuitive knowledge, it was empirical; unlike deduction, it yielded new knowledge of facts; unlike empiricism, it informed us not merely of what exists or occurs, and in what spatial or temporal order, but also why it is or occurs (i.e., its human motivations).

This species is self-knowledge, "knowledge of activities of which we, the knowing subjects, are ourselves the authors, endowed with motives, purposes, and a continuous social life, which we understand, as it were, from the inside."[1] Only here are we not passive observers, looking on from the outside as when we observe the external world, where all we can see is surface and not actual inner life and goals. Concerning nature, we can at best speculate about these inner goals. So the Baconian empiricists are right to say that, concerning the external world, we can only know what the senses report and that the best we can do is observe regularities and examine patterns. We are rightly restricted to explanation as observation. Our knowledge of humanity is different, however. We can indeed understand intentions and motivations. Here we can judge human activity in terms of purposes, motives, acts of will, decisions, doubts, hesitations, thoughts, hopes, fears, desires, and so forth. To apply these categories to nature is a mistake.[2] But to apply them to the study of human things is entirely legitimate.

It is important to note that Vico's critique of the scientific method is based on his Christian conception of creation. Vico argued that, made in God's image, we are creators of culture. Since we inhabit culture as its creators, our knowledge of cultural expressions in the fields of history, art, and literature has a different quality than scientific knowledge. Science we know from the outside, but humanistic knowledge is known by participation. We can understand human actions throughout his-

1. Isaiah Berlin, *Three Critics of the Enlightenment: Vico, Hamann, Herder*, ed. Henry Hardy (Princeton, NJ: Princeton University Press, 2000), 41.
    2. Ibid., 42.

tory because of a common spiritual bond as God's creatures. Vico's important point is that this knowledge is not somehow secondary to scientific knowledge but presents its own, fully valid kind of knowing. In fact, this "self-knowledge" is superior to scientific knowledge because it acquaints us with the movement of the human spirit through time and history and so helps us to understand and improve ourselves morally. Vico believed that this kind of knowledge, rather than scientific knowledge, would lead to the improvement of human society. He called this way of knowing "new science" or "new knowledge" (*scientia nuova*).

This new science analyzed divine reason as it worked itself out in human institutions. Its first principle was "a rational civil theology of divine providence . . . a demonstration, so to speak, of what providence has wrought in history, for it must be a history of the institutions by which without human discernment or counsel, and often against the deigns of men, providence has ordered this great city of the human race."[3] Since divine reason works through human agency, however, Vico's rational theology required the study of the human traditions in which we participate: "our Science proceeds by a severe analysis of human thoughts about the human necessities or utilities of social life." And so in its second main aspect, the New Science was therefore "a history of human ideas, on which it seems the metaphysics of the human mind must proceed." After all, argued Vico, "this world of nations has certainly been made by men, and its guise must therefore be found within the modifications of the human mind. And history cannot be more certain than when he who creates the things also narrates them."[4] Vico thus fused divine providence with human institutions from the analysis of which we can deduct universal principles concerning "a common sense of the human race." Vico concluded that "thus our science comes to be at once a history of the ideas, the customs, and the deeds of mankind. From these three we shall derive the principles of the history of human nature, which we shall show to be the principles of universal history."[5]

3. Giambattista Vico, *The New Science of Giambattista Vico*, 3rd ed. (1744), trans. Thomas Goddard Bergin and Max Harold Fisch (Ithaca and London: Cornell University Press, 1988), 102.

4. Ibid., 104.

5. Ibid., 113.

With this new science, <u>Vico became the father of our modern idea of the humanities.</u>[6]

But is not Vico's definition of the humanities itself a form of dualism? Did he also not separate the realm of nature and the realm of human studies and so help to establish the current split we see in our present universities between the humanities and the natural sciences? Why does such a dualist deserve positive mentioning in a book that argues against dualism? The answer to these justified questions is that good ideas that emerge in reaction to bad ones are not themselves perfect. This is not so much a weakness we can remedy but simply a fact of our historical, limited viewpoint. We can never assume a godlike stance of knowing things perfectly. Nor could Vico. In pointing out the limitations of scientific methodology and its unsuitability for the human sciences, Vico did enshrine the fateful distinction between explanation and understanding that still plagues knowledge theory today. As we will see later, it simply cannot be maintained that scientists restrict themselves to neutral observation whereas humanistic disciplines require imagination and emotional involvement in their research.

At the same time, however, Vico insisted on the deeply historical nature of human knowledge, and he anticipated the postmodern emphasis on the linguistic embodiment of reason. These ideas are very much connected to one another. In contrast to the Enlightenment, Vico did not believe that language and cultural expression in literature and art were just continually evolving expressions of the same universal, timeless truths. Vico denied a changeless structure of experience that could be perfectly reflected in pure mathematical language (if such could be invented). The "language of so-called primitives is not an imperfect rendering of what later generations will express more accurately; it embodies its own unique vision of the world, which can be grasped, but not translated totally into the language of another culture."[7]

We will see this important connection between language and worldview again in postmodern rejections of universal reason:

6. This modern term *humanismus*, is not a direct derivative of the Renaissance humanism, but rather a translation of the German term *Geisteswissenschaften*, the sciences of the human spirit, which pursue a different goal from the natural sciences (*Naturwissenschaften*).

7. Isaiah Berlin, *The Proper Study of Mankind: An Anthology of Essays*, ed. Henry Hardy and Roger Hausheer (London: Pimlico, 1998), 355.

human reason and truth are not ahistorical, timeless Platonic essences that somehow float above our reality; they are incarnated in time and history. This is why we have to work hard at understanding the connection between worldview and language, between cultural expression and ways of seeing.

Vico's belief in our ability to understand past human actions did not issue in the Enlightenment idea of human progress. His notion of human reason as bounded by history and linguistic expression provides a healthy antidote against the chronological snobbery of the Enlightenment, which tends to consider the modern/new as automatically more rational and therefore better. In contrast to the scientific humanism that the Enlightenment produced and that still is alive and well in many academic disciplines, Vico has a more balanced and humble view of human reason. Although he assumes a common rational human faculty on the basis of his belief in the divine image in us, he reminds us that reason is not some divine intuition but part of our historical, finite existence. Consequently, Vico's understanding of research in the humanities is already quite perspectival and interpretive whereas the rationalistic definition of truth—with its ideal of an unmediated, directly-evident-to-all-who-would-care-to-look kind of knowledge—trusts rather blindly in the power of human reason.

Vico's desire to qualify reason by criticizing Descartes's idea of timeless universal principles did not get a very wide hearing in the eighteenth and nineteenth centuries. Intellectuals in the West were having too much success making progress, especially technological progress, to question seriously the foundations of modern thought. This trust in abstract timeless reason, however, became the primary target of what has become known as the postmodern critique of the Enlightenment and, consequently, of secular scientific humanism as well. This critique, in some regards, works in concert with reservations Christian students ought to have about scientific objectivism, reservations expressed early on by the Christian humanist Vico.

Study Questions

1. Why should Christians lead the way in showing the limitations of the Enlightenment?

2. To challenge Descartes, Vico suggests a participatory model of knowledge, or self-knowledge. How is this model based on Christian principles? What is the goal of this "new science"?
3. To what extent do Vico's views on language and culture reflect the notion that truth is interpretation?
4. What are the limitations of Vico's critique of the Enlightenment?

7

NON-CHRISTIAN CRITICISM
OF ENLIGHTENMENT
HUMANISM

look, 3 philosophers
I HATE ☹

THIS CHAPTER FOCUSES ON THREE prominent non-Christian critics of the Enlightenment, often termed the masters of suspicion: Friedrich Nietzsche, Karl Marx, and Sigmund Freud. Nietzsche's rejection of timeless truths, Marx's unmasking of ideology, and Freud's attack on self-mastery each undermined the popular Enlightenment notion that we can construct an edifice of certain knowledge from universal rational principles. The final section of this chapter shows the culmination of these anti-Enlightenment impulses in the work of Martin Heidegger.

Introduction

Friedrich Nietzsche offers a supremely lucid, accessible, and devastating critique of the Enlightenment project. A discussion of the intellectual climate of the contemporary university moves easily between Nietzschean philosophy and two other dominating movements of the twentieth century, Marxism and psychoanalysis. Nietzsche stands between Karl Marx, who began writing about fifteen years earlier than him, and Sigmund Freud, whose life continued for a couple of generations after him. All three of these figures inculcated an attitude of suspicion regarding conventional views of morality, economics, and selfhood. Each of these "masters of suspicion" deserves careful and ample attention; taken together, their concerns serve to introduce those of contemporary intellectual culture. The academic environment of today's universities is still one of suspicion.

Nietzsche against the Enlightenment ⟶enough said

One of the most significant figures in the nineteenth century for critiquing the Enlightenment was the German philosopher Friedrich Nietzsche (1844–1900). He articulated a clear, uncompromising stance against the Enlightenment and remains widely influential on university campuses even today. He is especially relevant to Christian students because he laid at the feet of Christians so much of the blame for what he perceived to be intellectually wrong.

Nietzsche ridiculed the Enlightenment obsession with universal values and concepts that somehow hover in an eternal space untouched by time and history. Whether one celebrated reason as the guiding human power that enabled scientific empiricism or as the mental capacity that enabled one to deduce truths without dirtying one's hands with the world, Nietzsche despised the veneration of reason in all its forms. To him, the sanctity of reason was an illusion that constituted the essence of metaphysics. The celebration of reason always and inevitably manifested itself as an aversion to the body, history, time, change. In the name of universality, Western metaphysics always ended up in a dualism that pitted mind against spirit, soul against body, history against the eternal. Nietzsche argued that because of this dualism, we value ideas over people and, instead of enjoying the pleasures of life with its changes and challenges, we want to escape to a safe mental haven of unchanging principles—in short, we deny life.

Nietzsche believed that education was the worst perpetrator of this general tendency. We memorize and study concepts as if we had not made them up ourselves but as if they had dropped ready-made from the sky. Then we pass these concepts on to others and force them to do the same. "Education" is not thinking but mindless regurgitation of concepts devoid of life and historical understanding. In his attack on universal, ahistorical reason, Nietzsche did everything to expose our fear of history. He emphasized human finitude and limitations. In beautiful, poetic language he suggested that all of reality is like a metaphor, always pointing to something else at which we never arrive. Language exemplified the natural and the historical, the sensuous and the beguiling. One could, at best, play with language and recognize that it inevitably revealed human limitations; ultimately, language, like all of history, plays with you.

Nietzsche's interests in language and power contributed to his expression of a philosophy that came to be associated with nihilism: ultimately, there is nothing to believe in. Yet Nietzsche himself was not a nihilist in this way. For him, nihilism meant the denial of life. Nonthinking people enslaved to bureaucratic systems, spineless administrators of a highly regulated and technologized society—these were the nihilists for him. He called them "the last human beings." It is therefore not without irony that Nietzsche's thought has come to stand for nihilism, especially in Christian vocabulary, because Christians, whom Nietzsche accused of precisely this spineless, life-denying, nonthinking attitude, were for him a prime example of nihilism.

The son of a Lutheran minister, Nietzsche railed against Christian hypocrisy and a system of morality that he felt to be essentially antilife. In a penetrating analysis, he showed how Christian morality could prop up certain ideological interests, how it could be used to give some people power over others. For him, Christianity was an illusion perpetrated on people on a massive scale. The extent of Christianity's influence on the West, from Palestine to Rome, from Rome to the whole of Europe, in the East to Constantinople and beyond, and with the beginnings of modern missions in the nineteenth century to the ends of the earth: this is the enormity of the illusion Nietzsche has in mind.

It is an open question to what extent Nietzsche was justified in equating Christianity—particularly as he saw it practiced in nineteenth-century European society—with the denial of life and full humanity. His critique of modernity is valuable nonetheless for its uncompromising stance against dualism. His emphasis on the historical development of concepts and his insistence on our finitude as beings firmly embedded in time, culture, and tradition are a significant correction of Enlightenment errors. In this limited sense, therefore, Nietzsche can assist us in our quest for an incarnational view of human existence and for a humanism adequate to serve as the foundation of university culture.

The Other Masters of Suspicion

Nietzsche's views have widespread implications. Two other figures, Marx and Freud, thought along closely similar lines. Karl Marx (1818–1883) had written that religion was "the opiate of the people": drugs foster illusions. Marx concluded the *Communist Manifesto* by urging people to suspect all their assumptions because they had been decisively shaped by the presence of religion in their lives. Like Nietzsche, Marx emphasized that we are beings in history and time. Marx argued specifically against a German Enlightenment philosopher of tremendous influence in the nineteenth century who had taught that ideas are the foundation of human existence. Marx held, to the contrary, that "we ascend from earth to heaven." For him, human life is defined first of all by the biological and economical. Nietzsche said much the same thing, though with a different emphasis. Nietzsche focused on our morality and the need to embrace a full, sensuous life. By contrast, Marx's target was specifically our working life. His thought remains important because we tend to forget how deeply our modern outlook is shaped by an implicit understanding of economic goals and forces.

Between them, both Marx and Nietzsche bequeathed to our intellectual culture a handful of key terms. Among these, "ideology" has become immensely important in university culture. Ideology is commonly defined as follows:

> The concept "ideology" reflects the one discovery which emerged from political conflict, namely, that ruling groups can in their thinking become so intensively interest-bound to a situation that they are simply no longer able to see certain facts which would undermine their sense of domination. There is implicit in the word "ideology" the insight that in certain situations the collective unconscious of

certain groups obscures the real condition of society both to itself and to others and thereby stabilizes it.[1]

This definition makes sense against the backdrop of a culture of suspicion: ruling groups tend to look out for their own interests; they ignore certain facts that do not fit their understanding, until they no longer even see the problems. The concept of ideology naturally forms an important component of worldview. In today's universities, interest in tracking and unmasking ideology has become a major impetus.

The definition of ideology quoted above refers to the "collective unconscious" of groups. The term "unconscious" signals the relevance of psychoanalysis, which drew attention to the phenomenon of the unconscious. Sigmund Freud (1856–1939) influenced intellectual culture by removing another bastion of self-confidence, namely, our ability to understand ourselves. Marx had caused us to lose confidence in how we understood human existence from an economic point of view. He pointed out the problems that arise when we put ideas and ideological agendas before people and when work and relationships become governed by the use of money; Freud made us lose confidence in our sense of self-understanding and self-control. He suggested that we have drives and instincts that would turn us into quite different creatures were it not for governing influences both in our conscious selves and in society.

Just as Nietzsche and Marx attacked universals, so Freud showed that the self is not an isolated and stable consciousness that taps directly into a timeless reservoir of universal truths. The Enlightenment notion of reason depended heavily on a stable and predictable self; reason was the greatest identifying feature of such a self. This inner sanctuary turned out to be a thin veneer of civility over a deeply conflicted and unpredictable unconscious. Human behavior required interpretation. This is nothing new to Christians, who knew long before Freud that the heart above all things is deceitful (Jer. 17:9).

The cardinal insight of these three masters of suspicion, that reason is not a neutral, universal entity has shaped current aca-

1. Karl Mannheim, *Ideology and Utopia*, quoted in Robert Paul Wolff, "Beyond Tolerance," in *A Critique of Pure Tolerance*, ed. Robert Paul Wolff, Barrington Moore Jr., and Herbert Marcuse (Boston: Beacon, 1965), 39.

demic study. In the last thirty years, the unflinching application of suspicion has caused many academics virtually to dismiss humanism, and this critique has precipitated a widespread sense of crisis in the university. In dismissing humanism, some academics were merely trendy. Others, however, did so out of the genuine conviction that humanism itself was deeply implicated in a dehumanizing metaphysical worldview one could no longer hold with a good conscience. Nietzsche's critique of metaphysics pointed in this direction. That critique became stronger with the arguments of the German philosopher Martin Heidegger, who said more clearly than any modern thinker before him that all knowledge is indeed interpretation and not the product of disinterested rationality.

Martin Heidegger: Worldview and the Limits of Enlightenment Humanism

The German philosopher Martin Heidegger (1889–1976) built on Nietzsche's critique of reason to call into question the most basic assumptions we make about the nature of reality. In his influential work *Being and Time* (1927), he emphasized that humans are all interpretive beings and that our whole understanding of reality involves interpretation. His insistence on the interpretive nature of truth and knowledge was not at all an endorsement of subjectivism or relativism. On the contrary, Heidegger's entire project tried to overcome the subjectivism the Enlightenment had created by enthroning human reason—located in the autonomous self—as the judge of reality. Heidegger argued that, paradoxically, in its very desire for objective certainty, the Enlightenment's emphasis on human reason led to a thoroughly subjectivist view of human knowledge. The combined elements of rationalism and empiricism we have described in chapter four finally developed into an attitude of scientific objectivism that extended a scientific measure of empirically verifiable truth to all human knowledge. Now objective truth was only what could be verified in a test-tube, and human judgments concerning culture, tradition, morality, and religion were deemed subjective. Heidegger's philosophy wanted to overcome this division of truth into subjective and objective knowledge by advocating a more holistic view of human knowing.

Heidegger's challenge consisted in taking on the common notion of truth Western culture had inherited from Bacon and Descartes, namely, that all knowledge begins with unshakable facts, established either in the mind (Descartes) or by scientific experiment (Bacon), which we then appropriate and interpret. This view of reality, Heidegger argued, is obsessed with establishing objective truth but in actuality represents an objectivism that denies the authenticity of primary human experience. This scientific objectivism tries to tell us that, in effect, what we see, feel, and hear is never really reality; rather, what is real is what the microscope reveals underneath what we see, feel, and hear. We end up with a worldview that denies the fact that we always see things in an existential context that makes them meaningful for us. This objectivist worldview condemns interpretive elements vital for a properly human experience of the world, such as feeling, aspirations, and cultural and social components of knowledge, as merely subjective.

In challenging this subject-object dualism, Heidegger inverted the Enlightenment paradigm by claiming that we have real knowledge of objects not when we dissect them in the laboratory under the microscope but when we encounter them as something meaningful within the context of our lives. When you think of your car, for example, you do not primarily think of it as it is depicted in the owner's manual, as a collection of technical elements and how they work together; rather, you think of it first of all as the thing that takes you to work or the thing that is fun to drive. Advertising knows this well, which is why it does not sell you the technical details as much as the existential context you desire, by connecting the car to reliability or a certain lifestyle.

Heidegger's basic thesis is that truth and meaning are not facts we find in a test tube but are rather interpretations. Interpretation does not mean we simply make up the world but that we integrate into a meaningful context according to deep-seated presuppositions of what concerns us most the manifold experiences that constitute our lives. Many of Heidegger's early writings try to uncover the most basic concerns that shape how we see and order the world, and he finally came up with our concern for death as the most important of these.

Like Vico's new kind of knowledge, Heidegger's idea of knowledge was revolutionary because he denied science's definition of objective knowledge as the primary mode of perception. Human lives were always to be seen in the greater context of existence itself, of the world, and of other people. Meaning could not originate in the thinking subject but must be found outside it. Unlike Vico, however, who appealed to the image of God, Heidegger destabilized all forms of knowledge by decentering the subject. He did not tell us where exactly we should look for meaning; as a philosopher, Heidegger refused to point to God as the greater something from which we should derive value and meaning. Instead, as we shall see, he gestured vaguely toward something greater than our own minds and thoughts from which truth reveals itself to us, rather than us wresting it from things through scientific experiment; but he did say that the isolated mind or consciousness is *not* the starting point for knowledge and that reason defined as scientific objectivity impoverishes, even dehumanizes, our notion of truth.

Heidegger believed that humanism itself, with its emphasis on human autonomy and self-sufficiency, was deeply implicated in modernist notions that privileged a scientific outlook. In trying to secure human dignity, humanism committed the error of making the human mind the measure of all things and fell prey to a dualistic metaphysics, with its subjectivist blindness to how knowledge really works. Indeed, Heidegger went so far as to claim that this kind of humanism made it possible for technology and bureaucracy to take over our world. This might seem odd. Humanism was supposed to be about humans, not machines and faceless bureaucracies. How could humanism lead to these problems? Humanism, Heidegger contended, was merely another manifestation of the metaphysical thinking in which reality is subordinated to abstract ideas. Ideas can become disembodied, cut off from people.

Humanism can, in fact, contribute to an emphasis on technology. Formerly humanism, in both its Christian and non-Christian manifestations, believed in education as a means for mental discipline and character formation; in Heidegger's day, the humanities were retreating in favor of task-oriented, practical disciplines. The humanistic emphasis on self-knowledge through the study of human history and traditions gave way to courses in technology and business management that taught practical skills to aid the individual in finding a niche in the increasingly technologically oriented "real world." In his famous *Letter on Humanism* (1954),

Heidegger openly blamed humanism, with its definition of human beings as rational animals, for fragmenting our world. He argued that this definition had caused nothing but trouble and had led to the highly inhuman world we now inhabited. His analysis is all the more pertinent today. As much as technology has helped us, it also continues to fragment our existence. Is this process not dehumanizing?

Heidegger called for a more noble and humane definition of our humanity, one that turned our eyes away from ourselves and toward the greater context of existence. He tried to describe this larger sum of our human existence in the world, a sum that is greater than any one person and that somehow speaks to us, with the term "Being." Paradoxically, Heidegger was profoundly anti-humanist, but he rejected humanism only in the name of a higher calling, a humanism attentive to Being.

In unearthing how we could get to the point of divorcing ideas from people, Heidegger provides us with a first-class example of worldview thinking. We use worldview thinking in the same hermeneutical sense that Heidegger does in his work. That is, worldview thinking is not the theoretical formulation and conceptual comprehending of a worldview, "as if one had the phenomenon of existence under control and could grasp it by the conceptual means afforded to us by science."[2] Worldview thinking does, of course, entail concepts and definitions, but it can never be the detached contemplation of some system; rather, thinking always occurs in concrete historical situations, motivated by concrete sociopolitical intentions and goals, most of which are usually hidden and have to be unearthed in painstaking reflection.

The difficulty of such serious reflection is that worldview thinking is itself an enactment of our historical embodiment. Heidegger thought that true self-reflection can be meaningfully revealed only when the inquirer fully includes his or her own historical personal involvement.[3] Neither our way of seeing the world nor our present historical situation is something we fully control. He demonstrated that even concepts that seem deeply natural to us are in fact someone's interpretation of reality. He reminded us that

2. Martin Heidegger, "Anmerkungen zu Karl Jaspers," in *Wegmarken* (Gesamtaufgabe 9; Frankfurt: Vittorio Klostermann, 1996), 15.
3. Ibid., 42.

"whatever happens to us historical beings, happens because of a prior decision about the nature of truth that is not of our own making."[4] He suggested that we must come to understand the arrogant attitude of individualism and mastery over nature and our fellow human beings that characterizes our modern outlook. Heidegger was hopeful that a profound understanding of this spirit of technology might help us find our way back to a way of seeing life and reality as an interconnected whole for which humanity is responsible, instead of treating all things like items in a Wal-Mart, seeing their value only in their usefulness for our consumption.

Why is Heidegger so important? Because he attacked directly the Enlightenment's way of measuring truth and determining rationality. Something was considered rational and true when it could be examined neutrally and objectively. Objective knowledge had to be free from any personal involvement, such as private religious convictions or emotions. When scientific methodology achieves such dominance and oversteps its legitimate boundaries by making universal claims, it becomes a worldview, scientism rather than science, which is only one particular mode of inquiry.[5]

Scientists themselves have acknowledged Heidegger's views. A case in point is the renowned chemist Michael Polanyi (1891–1976). Polanyi taught that all knowledge, including scientific knowledge, depends on creativity and imagination. Without a creative imagination, the scientist would never come up with hypotheses and new ideas.[6] Instead, like any other experts, scientists depend on educated hunches.

Polanyi also confirmed Heidegger's point that scientific procedure, like any other mode of inquiry, relies on unquestioned assumptions. He observed that one fundamental, unquestioned,

---

4. Heidegger, "Platons Lehre von der Wahrheit," in *Wegmarken*, 237.

5. See, e.g., James Reimer's comments: "It is when scientific methodology is taken to be the only legitimate approach to knowledge, and when it becomes an all embracing worldview (scientism), in which no true knowledge is possible outside that which is empirically observable, that it threatens the true nature of the university" ("The Modern University," in *Mennonites and Classical Theology* [Kitchener, Ont.: Pandora, 2001], 101–26, here 110).

6. Michael Polanyi and Harry Prosch, *Meaning* (Chicago: University of Chicago Press, 1977), 59.

tacit assumption of science is, for example, a universe rational enough to make science possible. Such basics as measurements, computations, and algebraic equations make sense only within a predetermined framework that the scientist cannot question if he or she wants to arrive at any knowledge at all. The integration of isolated facts into a meaningful whole requires our personal commitment to these tacit frameworks.[7] Polanyi concluded that "two functions of the mind are jointly at work from the beginning to end of an inquiry. One is the deliberatively active power of the imagination; the other is a spontaneous process of integration which we may call *intuition*."[8]

Conclusion

The train of thought begun by Nietzsche and completed by Heidegger effectively wipes out Enlightenment dualism and the idea that scientific knowledge is superior to insights in the humanities. As Polanyi observed, "If personal participation and imagination are essentially involved in science as well as in the humanities, meanings created in the sciences stand in no more favoured relation to reality than do meanings created in the arts, in moral judgments, and in religion . . . since the dichotomy between facts and values no longer seems to be a real distinction upon which to hang any conclusion."[9]

Although Heidegger's call to a more holistic existence beyond Enlightenment humanism sounds very appealing, his antihumanism suffers from important weaknesses. From a theological perspective, Heidegger's acute criticism of modernity fails to provide a measure of discernment that allows for a true humanism. It is all well to claim that we need a more holistic outlook, but how do we measure the quality of this greater context? How can I know—to follow Heidegger's suggestion—that an organic, integrated world does not lead us back into paganism, undue veneration of nature, and the supremacy of the strong over the weak? An incarnational theology of the kind Aquinas pursued in the Middle Ages had a much better handle on this problematic.

7. Ibid., 61.
8. Ibid., 60 (emphasis original).
9. Ibid., 65.

Furthermore, although Heidegger provided perhaps the most penetrating philosophical analysis and criticism of modernity, the reception of his work by postmodern thinkers has done little to halt the fragmentation of the university. On the contrary, Heidegger's antihumanism in combination with the critique of the Enlightenment by Nietzsche, Marx, and Freud deeply affected humanism and the humanities. *Because humanism had accepted scientific principles, their attack on the scientific ideal of certain, impersonal knowledge amounted to an attack on humanism and humanistic learning at the same time.* When this attack becomes the dominant intellectual culture, we have arrived at postmodernism.

You presently participate in a university culture that is deeply affected by postmodernism, although its influence is slowly beginning to wane. The next section of this book is intended to familiarize you with the postmodern university and its relation to our humanist heritage. Postmodernism is often associated with nihilism and relativism, that is, the complete denial of meaning and of universally valid truth claims. Yet to understand postmodernism in the context of humanism in fact allows us to find postmodern elements that can help us in constructing a Christian, incarnational humanism. We call these elements "postmodern humanisms" because, like incarnational humanism, they seek to recover humanistic ideals without repeating the errors of the Enlightenment. In contrast to thinkers engaged in such a project, postmodernism also contains explicitly antihumanist thinkers who embrace the interpretive nature of truth but deny any greater context that would allow universal truth claims. Unfortunately, this more radical strand of postmodernism has largely shaped our current university culture.

Study Questions

1. When you read the names Marx, Nietzsche, and Freud, what comes to mind? What do the three have in common?
2. How do Nietzsche, Marx, and Freud each critique the Enlightenment, and why should Christians support their criticisms?
3. How does Heidegger challenge dualism? And humanism?

4. What do you think "worldview" means? How does your understanding differ from Heidegger's when he claims that a worldview is not a theoretical formulation?
5. How does Polanyi make worldview thinking and scientific thinking compatible?

POSTMODERNISM AND HUMANISM

8

POSTMODERN HUMANISM

"The only problem with humanism is that it's not human enough."

Emmanuel Levinas

THIS CHAPTER OFFERS AN INTRODUCTION to postmodernism by delineating its nobler, more humanist side. The postmodern philosophers Hans-Georg Gadamer and Emmanuel Levinas want to recover humanism for a post–World War II generation. Whereas Gadamer recovers the humanist ideal of self-knowledge and education for a post-Enlightenment university culture, Levinas asserts human dignity. His insistence on ethics has had a marked influence on the more radical postmodern thought presented in the next chapter.

Introduction

One of the most often asked questions in first-year humanities and interdisciplinary courses is, "Can you give me a definition

123

of postmodernism?" The standard answer is that, by definition, postmodernism has no definition, but this nonanswer is not very satisfying. Nor is it any longer true, as the large number of primers on postmodernism shows. Put simply, *post*modernism is the outlook that comes *after* modernism, that is, after the Enlightenment enthusiasm for a better future through reason and applied technology wanes.[1]

Postmodernism is both a break with and an extension of modernism. It breaks with modernism by denying grand stories that legitimate universal truth claims and by emphasizing the interpretive nature of truth. It also denies the idea of an autonomous self, an isolated inner mind as the starting point for our engagement of reality. Curiously, however, postmodernism uncritically adopts the Enlightenment prejudice against religion, particularly against the Christian faith. This blindness prevents postmodernists from recognizing the Christian story as the only grand narrative that by its very nature is not totalizing or oppressive (even though its followers may often give that impression).

This and the next chapter will attempt to define postmodernism by examining its relation to humanism. We first look at two postmodern thinkers who want to recover humanism. The first is the postmodern humanism of Hans Georg Gadamer, whose work is also known as hermeneutic philosophy[2] because he emphasizes the point that ideas for our interpretation of the world do not simply pop into our heads from nowhere but are passed on to us through tradition. The second postmodern figure is Emmanuel Levinas, who advocates a "humanism of the other human being" to criticize both modern and postmodern ideas of who we are.

The humanist postmodernism of Gadamer and Levinas crystallizes three predominant ideas: that the solitary thinking mind is a myth, that truth is interpretation, and that totalizing concepts or structures are to be refused on ethical grounds. These three ideas

---

1. You will also often hear the terms "modernity" and "postmodernity." Most people use them interchangeably with "modernism" and "postmodernism." Some academics, however, use the suffix "-ism" for the theoretical claims of each movement and reserve the suffix "-ity" for cultural manifestations of these theories.

2. "Hermeneutics" is a term derived from the Greek *hermeneuein*—"to interpret." Hermeneutics is simply the theory of interpretation. Hermeneutic philosophy, or philosophical hermeneutics, makes the claim that all thinking proceeds interpretively, that all knowledge is perspectival and hence requires hermeneutic reflection.

will help to form a fairly solid definition of postmodernity at the end of this chapter. The next chapter will focus on a more anti-humanistic strand of thought that has shaped current university culture. We easily misunderstand and underestimate postmodernism when we do not realize that it contains both humanist and antihumanist elements.

Gadamer's Recovery of Humanism: Education and Tradition

Martin Heidegger's student Hans-Georg Gadamer (1900–2002) agreed with his teacher on the interpretive nature of truth. He disagreed, however, with Heidegger's antihumanism. Like Hei-degger, Gadamer rejected the autonomous self of the Enlighten-ment and its objectivist notion of truth. But unlike Heidegger, Gadamer finds in classical humanism's emphasis on tradition and self-knowledge the very means to correct Enlightenment dualism. For Gadamer, reason and truth are not timeless concepts floating in some disembodied, timeless space but are concretely incarnated in this world. We can summarize his ideas briefly under two main aspects: education and tradition.

Gadamer argues that education is not primarily the storing up of facts but the movement away from one's own narrow horizon into the greater context of how people have thought concerning the great human questions throughout the ages. The main purpose of an education in the humanities is the surpassing of the self, a move from the particular toward the universal:

> It is not enough to observe more closely, to study a tradition more thoroughly, if there is not already a receptivity to the "otherness" of the work of art of the past. This is precisely what, following Hegel, we emphasized as the general characteristic of Bildung [education]: keeping oneself open to what is other—to other, more universal points of view. It [education] embraces a sense of proportion and distance in relation to itself, and hence consists in rising above itself to universality. To distance oneself from oneself, and from one's private purposes means to look at these in the way that others see them.[3]

3. Hans-Georg Gadamer, *Truth and Method*, 2nd rev. ed. (New York: Continuum, 1994), 17.

Thus humanism, for Gadamer, aims at universality, something
one achieves by broadening one's horizons, by going beyond the
particularity of our given nature and learning from others who
have transmitted to us the wealth of their wisdom.[4]

One can detect in Gadamer echoes of literary humanism's definition of education as moral progress through the formation of
responsible citizens. Moral progress means the capacity for self-
knowledge and self-correction. According to this model, university
education should allow you to orient yourself within the greater
tradition that constitutes and shapes our worldview. Gadamer
believes that the humanities provide such self-knowledge by which
we can find our spiritual-moral bearings relative to other cultures,
whereas science offers functional or technical knowledge. Even
though science, too, is shaped by a worldview, its does not usually
reflect critically on these deeper assumptions.

Consequently, the main resource of education is tradition. We
remember that Enlightenment thinkers had been deeply suspicious
of tradition. Tradition, they believed, meant blindly following
someone else's opinion. In their eagerness for intellectual freedom
from the abuse of tradition, however, they forgot that we can only
know *through* tradition. No tradition, no self-knowledge. Remember, too, that Heidegger had said that we cannot know without
deeper assumptions and predilections. Gadamer sharpens this
point by telling us that we obtain these presuppositions from our
respective intellectual and cultural traditions. He believes that even
what we consider our most pure inner space, our consciousness,
is shaped by history and tradition. Therefore, instead of rejecting
tradition, we should acknowledge and understand our tradition
in order to recognize why we think the way we do. We should
no longer *mis*use the motto "Dare to think!" to define ourselves
over against tradition because no one thinks in a vacuum. Instead
our intellectual outlook and cultural identity are shaped by the
tradition within which we move, live, and have our being.

For many of us, this is first of all the Western tradition of
thought shaped by the Greco-Roman and Judeo-Christian cultures.
Within this greater category, our nationalities, our upbringing, and

---

4. Jean Grondin, "Humanism and the Hermeneutical Limits of Rationality," in
Sources of Hermeneutics (New York: State University of New York Press, 1995),
130.

political and governmental educational policies shape who we are. None of these are prisons of ultimate determination, but they do delimit who we are. It is an important indicator of how deeply we are influenced by Enlightenment thinking that we feel threatened by this concept of tradition. We are so enamored of defining ourselves individualistically as a pure untouchable consciousness or mind first, and as a being in social relations second, that we do not like to face another possibility of selfhood. Gadamer's view of the self is more in line with the biblical idea that the self is determined by tradition and story and that ultimate self-certainty and clarity are illusory because the self is ultimately unknowable, to be known only by God.

How does tradition work? Tradition is passed on to us through oral and written texts. To acknowledge the value and necessity of tradition is also to recognize the importance of language. Much like the literary humanists mentioned earlier, Gadamer holds that words are not mere containers for ideas, that linguistic form and content go together. Language is no longer a secondary manifestation of the human spirit alongside art, law, and religion "but represents the sustaining medium of all of these manifestations of the spirit."[5]

For Gadamer, language is not merely something secondary, a crutch and memory device we need to record our thoughts, as if direct conversation would obviate the need for interpretation, but "the element in which we live, as fishes live in water."[6] Language is the preliminary medium that encompasses all beings insofar as they can be expressed in words. We do not simply control language like a tool but are surrounded by it. It is *within*, not merely through, language that we think, dream, and construct our world. Because language reflects the human spirit in time and history, we cannot simply learn concepts by heart and spit them back out in exams. We have to understand what they intend. For this reason careful study of texts and of the history of ideas and concepts within their social, historical environment is so important. This is why, for example, we cannot declare the King James

5. Hans-Georg Gadamer, "The Nature of Things," in *Philosophical Hermeneutics*, ed. and trans. David E. Linge (Berkeley: University of California Press, 1976), 76.
6. Hans-Georg Gadamer, "Reflections on My Philosophical Journey," in *The Philosophy of Hans-Georg Gadamer*, ed. Lewis Hahn (Chicago: Open Court, 1997), 22.

Version of the Bible the only true translation; time has moved on and we need to translate the meaning of the Bible for every major generational shift anew. This is because we live in language, and language forms us as much as we shape it.

Unlike radical postmodernists, Gadamer does not believe that the historical nature of truth issues in fragmentation and relativism. On the contrary, understanding between cultures, traditions, and therefore also academic disciplines is ultimately possible because all are expressions of human reason in different languages. Gadamer believed that because all human beings exist as linguistic beings, we can in principle translate every cultural expression into our own language. This requires that we learn other languages and cultural peculiarities.

In the end, however, every utterance can be translated and understood. Dialogue between people, cultures, and academic disciplines is always possible. For Gadamer, the task of education is to find a common language that would allow us to understand one another so that our different perspectives are fused and both parties understand first of all what they are actually talking about; even if they do not agree in their opinions, they should at least agree on the exact content of their conversation. This requires that we first listen carefully to another person or position and that we be ready to concede that perhaps the other person has it right.

Gadamer's recovery of humanism, with its insistence on education as acquiring self-knowledge on the basis of tradition, commends itself to incarnational humanism because of its emphasis on the incarnate nature of truth in culture and history. The problem with this humanism is its implicit assumption that we do in fact put the other first. Why should we not read into the text what we want? Why should we listen to our conversation partner, whether it is an ancient historical text, a novel, or the person next to us? What ethical imperative keeps me from slotting, objectivizing, and thus dehumanizing other traditions, opinions, and perspectives? And most important, how can we make human dignity the preeminent reference point for all human thought and action, a reference point that can never be changed by culture or tradition? This is the central question the Jewish philosopher Emmanuel Levinas has tried to answer.

Emmanuel Levinas's Ethical Humanism

Gadamer's recovery of humanism insists on the central role of reason and its human expression in time and culture. Education is essentially self-knowledge through the exploration of one's own and other traditions. The conclusion of Gadamer's humanism is that the cosmopolitan person who is well versed in culture and tradition is also the most reasonable and educated one. Good humanistic education turns to tradition to "constantly seek and rebuild culture."[7] Many have found this view of humanism too good to be true. Whose tradition and whose reason, after all, are we talking about?

These are also the questions of Emmanuel Levinas (1906–1995). Although Levinas agrees with Gadamer's criticism of Enlightenment philosophy, he sharply disagrees with the humanism Gadamer offers in its place. For Levinas, Gadamer's quintessential humanist belief that reading good books makes us better people is patently false, since it is often the most cultured people who commit the greatest atrocities. Gadamer's teacher Heidegger was a case in point: through philosophy, he legitimized his participation in the Nazi regime. For Levinas, neither modernist nor postmodernist humanism managed to secure human dignity as the most important element in education.

Levinas insists that neither Heidegger nor Gadamer was radical enough in his Enlightenment criticism. He believes that we will only recover humanism if we focus uncompromisingly on human beings. We must begin not with greater totalities such as Heidegger's Being or Gadamer's tradition but with our concrete social relation to other human beings. Philosophy does not come first in our reflections but the ethical relation to our fellow human being, and such a beginning is not Greek but Hebraic. It is in the Bible, argues Levinas, that we find the true ethical grounds for humanism: responsibility to one's neighbor. It is this ethical demand of the other human being that limits one's self-centered impulse for control over nature and others.

Levinas's importance for the recovery of humanism in the university lies in his insistence that ethics affects not merely how one lives but also how one thinks. He argues that the Greek infatuation

7. Grondin, "Humanism," 131.

with the mind as the starting point for all thought lies at the heart of the current crisis in the universities. Levinas cites the modernist and postmodernist intellectual development in the university as a tragic example and warning against the neglect of ethics as the foundation of knowledge. For example, with the disappearance of the self in extreme forms of postmodern antihumanism, knowledge itself has become meaningless. For him, the current crisis of postsecondary education demonstrates the urgent need to uphold the absolute, unique value of the ethical human relation as the measure of all things.

Levinas reminds us that humanism was founded on the concept of human dignity, essential for all human intellectual and social activity. His concern is that the death of the human subject, which dominated philosophical discourse in the human sciences, inevitably entailed the death of human dignity and thus opened the gates for inhumane atrocities. Levinas does not miss the deep irony that research in the humanities has focused on the death of the human and found renewal and strength in a number of obituaries: the end of humanism and the end of metaphysics, the death of the human and the death of God.[8]

Levinas argues that neither the Enlightenment nor its postmodern critics managed to provide us with a truly human idea of who we are and how we know. Whereas secular scientific humanist conceptions of the self and of knowledge aimed to establish the human subject as an autonomous will who masters his or her environment, the postmodern critique of modernity culminated in the exact opposite by resolving the self into its shaping influences. Modernist humanism emphasized individuality, but in fact it produced not individuals but clones of universal reason. The very tolerance of the Enlightenment was premised on the idea that we should all have the same political and intellectual ideas.

Levinas proposes instead to ensure human dignity and prevent the dangers of modern and postmodern philosophy by making the other person's ethical claim on my existence the most important element for our thinking and acting. For Levinas, all research, knowledge, writing, and art must have as its ultimate goal the welfare of one's neighbor. In other words, Levinas provides edu-

8. Emmanuel Levinas, *Humanismus des anderen Menschen* (Hamburg: Felix Meiner, 1989), 85.

cation with a much needed ethical framework, and he does so by calling for the restoration of the biblical, Hebraic tradition of thinking, which had been and remains all but dismissed from university culture. Only here, he claims, do we find a radically ethical starting point for thought and action.

Postmodern Tensions

Gadamer and Levinas represent the humanist arm of postmodern thinking. They help us recover an earlier humanistic foundation of university studies. Heidegger had shown that our thinking is too much framed by a technological stance of mastery from which we see all things as instruments, including human beings. Gadamer had refined this thought to emphasize the importance of education as self-knowledge through tradition. Both were convinced that we have lost the ability to see the intrinsic value of things. Levinas adds the important insight that education fails if it does not recognize the intrinsic value of humanness.

Even the briefest comparison of Gadamer's hermeneutic humanism and Levinas's "humanism of the other human being" reveals a basic tension within postmodernism between the particular and the universal. The deep postmodern suspicion against totalizing, dehumanizing systems stands in agonizing opposition to the yearning to overcome fragmentation by emphasizing the value of tradition and community for self-knowledge. Suspicion of systems is reflected in Levinas's emphasis on radical difference or otherness; desire for community is represented by Gadamer's insistence that we know nothing in isolation from tradition. Where Gadamer emphasizes the commonalities we have with other people across time, Levinas emphasizes the uniqueness of every voice. Where Gadamer emphasizes similarity and integration in education, Levinas champions difference and particularity. Where Gadamer would seek to find common voices and ideas in a tradition, Levinas thinks that traditions are formed by the dominant majority to the exclusion of others.

Levinas's ethical concern is important, and it forms indeed the core of much postmodern thought. Postmodernism remains misunderstood if we do not recognize this. We must now add to our earlier definition of postmodernism that it is an *ethical* movement.

Following Levinas, the ethics of postmodernism lie precisely in its absolute hatred (no weaker word seems justified) of objectifying human beings according to some theoretical system. Whenever we erect such a system, even if it is with good intentions (such as Marxism or Christianity or humanism), we run the danger of explaining away uniqueness in the name of universal values and will soon begin to oppress those who do not fit our preconceived schema. *Contrary to popular opinion, the heart of postmodernism is not a desire for relativism (even though much of our popular postmodern culture is characterized by just such a wish) but rather an obsession with responsibility to recognize others as different from ourselves.*

For example, Jacques Derrida, the father of a postmodern form of radical inquiry called deconstruction, claims ethics as the primary impulse behind his thinking. Deconstruction is a form of justice that allows another's opinion full value and deconstructs all totalizing systems of thought that would easily objectify others by putting them into an intellectual box in order to classify, anticipate, and then dismiss them. Defending himself against the charge of relativism and meaninglessness, Derrida avows that "deconstruction is not a form of nothingness but an openness toward the other."[9] → nutcase

Conclusion

In their mutual attack on scientific humanism, Gadamer's and Levinas's postmodern humanisms emphasize respectively the interpretive nature of truth and the importance of human dignity. Gadamer tells us that knowledge and intellectual growth occur in community; Levinas asserts that human identity and knowledge exist only in service to my neighbor. Since tradition and systematized knowledge tend to objectify others or, even worse, classify who is and who is not my neighbor, Levinas is suspicious of Gadamer's hermeneutics with its emphasis on tradition. Whose tradition, after all, are we talking about? How can we evaluate tradition itself?

9. Richard Kearney, *States of Mind* (New York: New York University Press, 1995), 173.

This suspicion of any instinct to universalize characterizes the second strand of postmodernism we now turn to. We call this second attitude antihumanism, and its main characteristic is fragmentation rather than coherence. It differs from Levinasian post-modern humanism in that, until very recently, it has ignored ethics. Instead it has redescribed framentariness as power relations. This deep suspicion of coherent accounts of meaning and reality, together with an insistence on perceiving all subject matter and all modes of inquiry as expressions of power, has extensively shaped the current university environment.

Study Questions

1. Do you care about postmodernism? Do you think you should care about postmodernism? Why or why not?
2. Why does Gadamer care about humanism?
3. How does Gadamer's humanism resemble pre-Enlightenment humanisms in terms of language and tradition?
4. In what ways do Gadamer's concerns suggest a postmodern humanism?
5. Why does Levinas care about humanism?
6. How does Levinas's humanism differ from Gadamer's in terms of his critique of secular scientific humanism?
7. How are Gadamer's and Levinas's postmodernisms ethically oriented?

9

POSTMODERN ANTIHUMANISM
AND THE UNIVERSITY

THIS CHAPTER INTRODUCES POSTMODERN ANTIHUMAN-
ISM, which has extensively shaped the research and curricular
agendas of the postmodern university. Its interests and programs
reflect the deep suspicion toward grand stories, called metanarratives, by which we legitimize what counts as valid knowledge.
The chapter will explain the origin and main conclusions of antihumanist postmodernism and then describe how it has shaped
the emphases of current university education.

Introduction

Whereas postmodern humanism is motivated primarily by the
deep human desire for meaning and thus for some kind of coherence and purpose to human knowledge, antihumanism regards this
very desire as dangerous. What many newcomers to postmodernist
ideas do not understand is that postmodern antihumanists do not
regard the absence of meaning and purpose as a tragedy but as an
opportunity that is to be celebrated. In this Nietzschean strand

of postmodernism, the dissolution of any stable notion of self-hood is seen as liberating because I can now invent myself, shape my own identity. According to this view, the absence of grand stories with their universally valid truth claims is not a loss but ultimate freedom, the freedom of every community to celebrate its own particular beliefs or religion. The following brief analysis of postmodern antihumanism introduces you to two of its main representatives, Michel Foucault and Jean-François Lyotard, to help you understand this particular worldview.

Michel Foucault's Antihumanism, or the "Dice Box of Chance"

Perhaps no other postmodern antihumanist more aptly demonstrates how deeply postmodern concerns are driven by the modernist ethos of reflection as liberation from authority than Michel Foucault (1926–1984). Foucault's research was motivated by the desire for freedom, and we are free when we recognize how things really are. This is why critical thinking is so important: it sets us free. Foucault wanted to engage in the kind of thinking "that allows us to free ourselves from ourselves. And instead of simply justifying what one already knows, what would happen if [the work of thinking] should succumb to the arduous task of endeavouring to know how it becomes possible to think differently?"[1]

In order to think differently, we have to examine our own worldview in its historical development and context. In Foucault's work we thus meet again the basic notion that nothing we know simply originates in some deep pure place within us but rather that we receive our ideas from our cultural environment. Thus Foucault was deeply interested in the social origins of our knowledge in the "fundamental codes of culture."[2] His desire for freedom is modern; his awareness of cultural embeddedness is postmodern.

There is nothing inherently wrong or antihumanist in recognizing the social dimensions of our knowledge. What makes Foucault's historical analysis of the origin of even our most profound ideals about what is good, true, and beautiful antihumanistic, however,

1. Michel Foucault, *The History of Sexuality*, vol. 2, *The Use of Pleasure* (New York: Vintage, 1990), 15.
2. Michel Foucault, *The Order of Things* (New York: Routledge, 2001), 381.

is his insistence that we can have absolutely no direction or norm to judge one historical opinion over another. The reason for this refusal is that Foucault was a disciple of Nietzsche, with whom he rejected any coherent attempt to tell the human story. Like Nietzsche, Foucault rejected any belief in definite trajectories or greater ends in history. Lofty concepts such as universal human reason are mere "inventions of the ruling class."[3] They inevitably reveal the exercise of power.

This last remark reveals one of Foucault's favorite themes, namely, that many of our social and institutional practices do not originate in deep eternal truths, written in our hearts and minds by the hand of some divinity, but are preferences imposed on society by its dominant members. What all of this boils down to is the complete absence of any direction or norm for historical or any other analysis or thinking. Foucault's worldview, which he terms "the world of effective history," is pretty much a Nietzschean one: "The inverse of a Christian world, spun entirely by a divine spider, and different from the world of the Greeks, divided between the realm of will and the great cosmic folly, the world of effective history [i.e., Foucault's worldview] knows only one kingdom, without providence or final cause, where there is only 'the iron hand of necessity shaking the dice box of chance.'"[4]

For Foucault, research and critical reflection resemble the work of an archaeologist who sifts through historical records without any ultimate reference point concerning their meaning. There simply is no deep meaning in history. The best we can and should do is to find out what historical influences make us think and act the way we do. From Foucault's analysis follow two conclusions that have shaped current university culture: first, that humanism is a sham and, second, that who we are and what we count as knowledge are determined by power relations.

It is not hard to imagine why Foucault is against humanism. For him, humanism represents the entire gamut of ideals he rejects: universal reason, ultimate meaning, the desire to establish a norm for self-improvement, and the need to link interpretation to a universal story to make sense of our lives. For Foucault, the

3. Michel Foucault, "Nietzsche, Genealogy, and History," in *The Foucault Reader*, ed. Paul Rabinow (New York: Pantheon, 1984), 142.

4. Ibid., 381.

ideal of freedom, *Sapere aude!* stands in opposition to humanism. The latter strives too much to define itself according to principles borrowed from disciplines such as religion, science, or politics whereas Foucault places all the emphasis on the power and limitations of the human will.[5]

Foucault insisted that humanism itself has hindered us from realizing that all our perceptions of reality are shaped by institutional practices that are advertised as humanistic but in fact marginalize those who do not conform to institutional ideals. Moreover, these ideals are themselves not eternally valid revelations of universal reason; rather, who we are and what we value are completely reducible to historically developed conventions. These include the idea that we somehow must have a measure for our humanity. What it means to be human cannot ever be answered.

The best we can do is to collect all possible interpretations of human nature and chart its development. Even interpretation as appropriation of tradition, the very things Gadamer's postmodern humanism had valued so highly, Foucault reduces to the ashes of meaninglessness. Within his "dice box of chance," Foucault's chain of reasoning is quite logical: interpretation is merely the "violent and surreptitious appropriation of a system of rules, which in itself has no essential meaning, in order to impose a direction, to bend it to a new will." What we view as the development of self-understanding concerning our human nature becomes merely a series of interpretations, the validity of which we can never ascertain. The same is true of any other humanist ideal.

With the postmodern humanist, the antihumanist embraces the interpretive nature of truth, but the latter gives up hope of any coherent meaning. Here we find the relativism so much heard of: "If interpretation is a never-ending task, it is simply because there is nothing to interpret. There is nothing absolutely primary to interpret, because when it is all said and done, underneath it all everything is already interpretation."[6] We may well ask why we should pursue learning at all. When pressed on this issue, the best Foucault can come up

5. Michel Foucault, "What Is Enlightenment?" in *Ethics: Subjectivity and Truth,* ed. Paul Rabinow, trans. Catherine Porter (New York: New Press, 1997), 313.

6. Michel Foucault, "Nietzsche, Freud, Marx," in *Michel Foucault: Essential Works of Foucault 1954–1984: Aesthetics, Method, and Epistemology,* ed. James D. Fabion and Paul Rabinow, trans. Robert Hurley et al. (New York: New Press, 1998), 275.

with is the need to identify what is dangerous to us. He argues that we need to understand the power relations that generate our values. Intrigued by Nietzsche's notion that all of existence is essentially a struggle for power, much of Foucault's work examines how power relations shape our social identity and institutions. He concludes that political and economic power struggles rather than abstract ideals explain who we are and what we believe in. These power relations also influence what we believe to be worthy of study. In other words, what gets taught in universities is determined by the general struggle for power that pervades all of human existence. To identify power relations can help us identify what is dangerous for us.

Yet in the absence of any universally valid guideline for our humanity, such tentative assertions of avoiding danger are rather futile. In order to identify dangers to our humanity, we have to know also what our humanity is meant to be. Yet such knowledge is impossible in Foucault's deeply fragmented world. Still, as we can see in the next antihumanist thinker, fragmentation was valued as a creative force.

Jean-François Lyotard and Creative Difference

When the Quebec government's council of universities requested a report on the state of knowledge in higher education, Jean-François Lyotard (1924–1998) published the desired account as *The Postmodern Condition* (1979). His main thesis was that universities should shift from a modernist conception of knowledge to a postmodern one. The premise for this demand was Lyotard's critique of scientific methodology. Lyotard attacks science because it is not scientific enough. His postmodernism amounts to an intensification of modernism. Science, he argues, has customarily defined itself over against religious and humanistic knowledge by pointing out that the neutral stance of science rejects all greater stories in its research. In religious cultures, these narratives "define what has the right to be said and done in the culture in question, and since they are themselves a part of that culture, they are legitimated by the simple fact that they do what they do."[7] Science, by

7. Jean-François Lyotard, *The Postmodern Condition* (Minneapolis: University of Minnesota Press, 1984), 23.

contrast, has defined itself against such self-legitimizing narratives. Its language is denotative rather than narrative. In short, science has dedicated itself to an ideal of truth set apart from narrative (which forms social bonds), which it associates with ignorance, barbarity, prejudice, superstition, and ideology.[8]

This means, however, that unlike narrative discourse, science cannot legitimate itself by its own performance (this is right because this is what we do); it has to appeal to an authority outside its own method to answer this question: "Why should there be scientific activity at all, and why should societies support scientific institutions of knowledge?" At this point, science itself turns to narrative for legitimation, namely, to political and philosophical narratives. Politically, science buys into the Enlightenment dream of the gradual emancipation of humanity from slavery and class oppression through the democratization of knowledge and technology. Philosophically, science partakes of the Enlightenment idea of an ever-expanding human maturity. Thus science, in contrast to its claim an objective fact-finding mission, legitimizes itself by adopting a grand story, the political and philosophical narratives of the Enlightenment, which are teleological, tending toward some final goal.[9]

Ironically, then, science uses narratives to legitimate its own project against so-called primitive narratives. In the twentieth century, however, the political and philosophical metanarratives of the Enlightenment became unbelievable. Lyotard vaguely explains this incredulity toward metanarratives as caused by the renewal of the spirit of capitalist free enterprise and the demise of communism. The growth of technologies in science has further encouraged a shift from ends to means, so that the metanarrative of science as a story of progress and enlightenment has become incredible. Whatever the cause may be, with the demise of the Enlightenment dream, the organizing power of science itself has weakened. It has lost its legitimizing metanarrative, the kind of narrative that science always put in place over and against belief, whether implicitly or explicitly. Science has devolved into a myriad of special areas, each with its own incompatible code of language games; each specialty is judged only on pragmatic grounds: what

8. Ibid., 27.
9. Ibid., 31–37.

works best (best defined in terms of self-proliferation, spawning more research along the same lines).

Lyotard does not see this fragmentation as problematic, but as a grand opportunity. Although science is now virtually reduced to sheer performance without any greater coherent goal for its research, this productivity may not only contain innovative energies but indeed encourage unorthodox leaps out of existing paradigms and new creativity. Science, argues Lyotard, should give up any pretense of coherence and celebrate creative difference. In a postmodern world, innovations will have to be made on the basis of creativity, rearranging in a new, unforeseen way the information known to all.

The Postmodern University

With the antihumanist strand of postmodern thought, the limits of reason and the interpretive nature of truth take a nasty turn toward utter fragmentation. As a result, the focus of research and scholarship in the postmodern university changes from great holistic schemes and overarching stories that legitimate particular research projects to particularities, to the sociopolitical dimensions of knowledge, and to the disavowal of the existence of great ends to or motivations for learning. We have arrived at the point where the learned professor in the introduction to this book can say, "I have no idea why I teach what I teach." At best, the university as a whole can model itself on Lyotard's creative difference, so that the only motivation for teaching is to generate creative differences without any greater sense of our humanity whatever.[10]

Without humanism as the glue that orients the various disciplines toward a common goal, the university has become deeply fragmented. Dualism is still entrenched in the customary opposition of the arts and the sciences, and the most obvious winners in the new environment are "practical" disciplines such as business, technical courses, and professional training programs. In the

10. This clearly is Richard Rorty's position, according to whom universities should "offer a blend of specialized vocational training and provocation to self-creation." This self-creation should produce individuals who can shape society a little bit differently from the preceding generation ("Education as Socialization and as Individualization," in *Philosophy and Social Hope* [London: Penguin, 1999], 123–24).

absence of other motivations, pragmatic materialism will always provide one. Even in the arts and sciences, the ever-increasing information overload has contributed to ever greater fragmentation and specialization of the disciplines. You can busy yourself obtaining the training to make a lot of money to buy all the modern conveniences; you can train yourself to be so busy that you never have time to ask yourself what it is all for. But if this is the purpose of the contemporary university, then it has totally lost sight of its original calling.

Although the postmodern attacks on secular humanism have necessarily and rightfully called science into question as a comprehensive worldview, these challenges have only exacerbated the fragmentation between disciplines that began with Enlightenment dualism. Academics no longer want to say anything general. Many have become specialists who dare not connect the dots between their insights to draw a larger picture.

The tendency to emphasize politics and power relations has become the primary focus. It is divorced from a sense of ethical responsibility to contribute to a larger story, and from any evident interest in individuals as human beings, precisely because of the lack of agreement about a core human identity. Many academics have turned on each other and have come to assume that one studies a subject not out of love but out of self-interest; many take for granted that the institution needs to coerce individuals into conforming to certain standards. The most public manifestation of this development in the 1980s and 1990s was the hideous parody of the intellectual life known as political correctness.

Emphasis on specifics has led to intellectual and moral timidity. So-called intellectuals have become reluctant to analyze rationally, to recognize patterns, to act in the world on the basis of generalized principles and insights gained from reflection. Instead they concentrate on particularities and differences and laud as intellectually rigorous the cynical critiques of pattern making and proposed narratives. Generalizations are equated with intolerance, manifestations of totalizing power. This tendency has led to an inadequate picture of what it means to be human.

These issues profoundly shape teaching in the contemporary university. The very idea of teaching goes against the grain of antihumanist assumptions because *the impulse to shape according to a model that can be shared by all is intrinsic to education.* Under antihumanism, students are left to sort things out on their own, not because they are being trained in independent critical thinking but because no one wants to presume to engage in intellectual, let alone moral and spiritual, formation. At the very least, students deserve a clearer explanation of the issues and why they should not confuse being in charge of their education with getting one.

Attacks on Christianity stemming from the Enlightenment are complicit in these developments. Unrelenting skepticism results in the absence of common points of reference. The attack on religion, an attack that dates from the Enlightenment, was once gleefully praised as the work of the worm of doubt.[11] As we have seen, Christians contributed to both the growth of university life and to changes that encouraged dualism. In the aftermath of the loss of belief, the question of what it means to be human became bound up with the acceptance of strict limits placed upon what we can say we know: Enlightenment humanism replaced religion. After this worm of doubt had eaten a hole through the apple of religion, it turned on belief in humanity itself. By the middle of the twentieth century, secular humanism found itself being dismantled by its own unrelenting spirit of inquiry. With reason discredited as the will to power and with religion consigned to the scrap heap of irrationality, the contemporary university is indeed in a crisis.

Conclusion

In the wake of the postmodern deconstruction of Enlightenment humanism, the university is marked by a crisis because we have lost the humanistic goal of university education. When is the last time you heard about character formation in the university? Or about the pursuit of virtue? Even the welcome current tendency toward interdisciplinary research makes sense only if we have a rough idea toward what overall end this effort tends. Interdisciplinarity cannot by itself remedy fragmentation; if we do not talk about what kind of human society research should serve, why conduct it? What we are left with after postmodernity is a crisis

11. Friedrich Nietzsche, *The Gay Science*, trans. Walter Kaufmann (New York: Random House, 1974), §122.

concerning the role of the university as a center for research and
the dissemination of knowledge.

This does not mean, however, that the postmodern university
is all bad. Cultural studies remind us that we are indeed dependent on history and tradition for our ideas. Feminism and gender studies testify to our need for identity-oriented studies, and
interdisciplinarity affirms our recognition of reality's complexity. Unfortunately, these laudable trends become destructive and
dehumanizing in the absence of a greater goal. Shaped largely
by antihumanist forces, the postmodern university culture lacks
what traditional humanism possessed: a common ideal of what it
means to be human that can ground our quest for self-knowledge
and give it direction.

As we have seen, even the best postmodern attempts to recover humanism fail. Gadamer's hermeneutical approach has the
right emphasis on education as self-knowledge and on the value
of tradition, but even he cannot offer an ethical dimension that
transcends culture and so allows us a universal idea of what it
means to be human.

Levinas and, with him, all ethically concerned postmoderns, on
the other hand, shelter their ethics of difference and uniqueness so
jealously from history and language that it is of little value. Here
every text, every concept or assertion is already an ethical violence.
Although these postmodern humanisms contain much that is attractive, the absence of a common measure of our humanity that is
firmly rooted in history and yet also transcends it looms large; the
antihumanist admission that truth and meaning are up for grabs
turns out to be more honest, unless, of course, we can imagine a
humanism that provides a universal measure of humanity from
within history, a measure that assures human dignity beyond all
historical change and yet is itself incarnated in history. We contend
that there is such a humanism, an incarnational humanism. As
a Christian student, you have the best resources for intellectual
inquiry at hand in the rudiments of your Christian theology.

Study Questions

1. How might the goals of coherence and purpose for human
   knowledge be misguided?

2. Why and how does Foucault define the goal of *Sapere aude!* in opposition to humanism?
3. How does Foucault, as a postmodern antihumanist, differ from the postmodern humanists described in the last chapter on the interpretive nature of truth?
4. How does Lyotard's critique of metanarratives undermine the Enlightenment story of science as superior to religion?
5. According to the authors, which of the two strands of postmodernism—postmodern humanism or postmodern antihumanism—has had the greater influence on the intellectual environment of the contemporary university?

10

INCARNATIONAL HUMANISM

T HIS CHAPTER PRESENTS OUR MAIN thesis: only the incarnation enables a recovery of humanism as the heart of university education because the incarnation allows us to retain the best elements of the greater humanist tradition *and* of its postmodern critics without repeating their shortcomings. Human dignity, the dignity of nature, and the interpretive nature of truth become possible without fragmentation or totalization. Thus incarnational humanism allows for considerable common ground with postmodern scholarship even as it maintains a distinctively Christian orientation.

Introduction

You have in basic Christian doctrine superlative resources for fulfilling the mandate of university education. The doctrine of the incarnation is as basic to Christianity as the Christmas story, and it has compelling and validating implications for the life of the mind.

Dualism, the separation of essential elements of our humanity, has emerged as the main problem in the history of humanism and therefore of university education. This book has shown you how most forms of humanism, even Christian ones, have fallen prey to dualism. It has also presented you with the best postmodern attempts to overcome dualism, which often fall into an extreme of either fragmentation or a rather fuzzy holism without any definite contours of what it means to be human. We will now explore how the Christian doctrine of the incarnation provides a model for a holistic humanism without dualism.

The Foundation of True Humanism: The Incarnation

In Jesus's incarnation, God entered into and identified with the perplexities of being human, of lived experience in a given time and a given place. Christians hold, as an article of faith, that the second person of the Trinity, the divine Logos, through whom creation was accomplished, has become human in time and history without sustaining any loss to divine transcendence.

When we unpack this idea of transcendence, we begin to see why the incarnation announces the end of all dualisms. In joining the words "Logos" and "flesh," John's Gospel writes intentionally against both Greek and Jewish dualisms. For the Greek mind, the term "Logos" denoted the power of reason that undergirded all of creation. Many Greek thinkers associated reason with the divine, which they defined as the unchangeable stability of the eternal in contrast with inferior physical matter that was subject to change and decay. The Jews in John's audience would have understood "Logos" to mean the word of God, God's power to create the world and to transform God's people through divine intervention. Yet to the Jewish mind, this God was so transcendent, his difference or otherness so extreme, that no one could see God's face and live.[1]

This book has shown how ideas and worldviews are intrinsically connected to language. John's Gospel showcases the power and importance of language to shape our worldview. By choosing the Greek term "Logos" to express the Jewish idea of God's word and wisdom, the author of John fuses two cultural frameworks or worldviews into a new, much richer one. In combining, building on,

1. Levinas's ethics of pure otherness or difference as justice derives from this theological concept, and its problems, too, find their solution in the incarnation.

and surpassing the Greek and Jewish traditions, John's interpretation of God's self-revelation overcomes their respective dualisms.

The incarnation remedies Greek dualistic thinking by fusing the realms of history and pure rationality. Moreover, since the incarnation means that the fullness of God dwells in the person of Jesus, it also goes beyond the Jewish notion of divine transcendence as unapproachable otherness. In the God-man the wholly other divine nature, so radically different from us, has become human sameness (humanity, history, language) without compromising its integrity. Armed with this concept, Christianity announces its opposition to dualism. For the Christian, all spheres of human existence and creation are united in Christ. The apostle Paul articulates fully what we find outlined in the Gospel of John:

> He is the image of the invisible God, the firstborn over all creation. For by him all things were created: things in heaven and on earth, visible and invisible, whether thrones or powers or rulers or authorities; all things were created by him and for him. He is before all things, and in him all things hold together. . . . For God was pleased to have all his fullness dwell in him, and through him to reconcile to himself all things, whether things on earth or things in heaven, by making peace through his blood, shed on the cross. (Colossians 1:15–20)

You cannot be more holistic than this. In Christ, all fragmentation ends and a new humanity begins, a new creation in which all knowledge is united (or taken captive, as Paul puts it) under the lordship of Christ because in him the divine and the human are firmly joined forever.

Incarnational humanism harnesses this idea for the recovery of humanism as the foundation of university education. We can now recover and affirm the central humanistic elements, human dignity and that of nature, from previous chapters in full recognition of their postmodern critique.

First, God's becoming human affirms the intrinsic worth of human existence. The whole purpose of the incarnation is to restore humanity to the image of God that was shattered by the fall, yet restoration implies also that all human beings are made in this image and are therefore intrinsically valuable. This universal value is, however, not a totalizing one that eradicates all differences in order to produce Christian clones.

The specific nature of God's image in us has been a long-standing debate within the Christian tradition. Gender, moral uprightness, unimpeded reason, the soul and its faculties, Christlikeness—all of these have been suggested. We may consider and explore any or all of these options as long as we follow a trinitarian model. The incarnation shows us a triune God in whom complete harmony of will and desire coexists with difference. The apostle Paul suggests something like this when he speaks of the church as a unified body with diverse parts.[2]

The church is supposed to represent the beginnings of humanity restored to communion with God. This new humanity, which lives in anticipation of its complete redemption upon Christ's return, is itself an image of the Trinity's unity in diversity. Jesus's promise that "you will realize that I am in my Father, and you are in me, and I am in you"[3] forms the spiritual-existential basis for our new humanity. This experience of unity contains, just as it did from the beginning, the diversity of male and female experiences. The Catholic theologian Hans Urs von Balthasar, for example, argues that the overall form of the Christian faith as lived out in the church is made up of the diverse Christ experiences of its founding figures. These four "archetypical" experiences of God's grace differ depending on their apostolic recipients. Peter's writings, for example, bear the mark of Christ's personal, postresurrection request that Peter feed his sheep.[4] Paul, by contrast, has a greater eschatological emphasis based on his own Damascus experience, detached from spending time with Christ during the normal course of his earthly life. In Paul, the experience of grace is our new humanity already in existence with Christ, awaiting its eschatological unveiling.[5] The apostle John's experience is particularly communal and incarnational, emphasizing the oneness of the church whose motivation is the comprehensive understanding of Christ from the incarnation and the cross to Christ's absolute rule in the apocalypse.[6] Thus to measure human dignity according to the divine image is not a reductive narrowing move but one that acknowledges the whole person with all his or her unique abilities

---

2. 1 Corinthians 12:12–29.
3. John 14:20.
4. Hans Urs von Balthasar, *Herrlichkeit: eine theologische Ästhetik* (Einsiedeln: Johannes Verlag, 1960), 1:340.
5. *Herrlichkeit*, 1:342.
6. *Herrlichkeit*, 1:349.

as worthy of our love and attention. In fact, it is the Christian's task to look at every person as potentially restored to the image of God, as if he or she could be a new creation in Christ.[7]

The fourth archetypical experience is that of Mary, whose experience of carrying the Christ—the complete giving of her being in service to God—forms for von Balthasar the framework for all Christian experience. The experience of motherhood in conjunction with the incarnation of God gives birth to the essential dynamic of the Christian faith: Mary opens herself up to God because of divine grace toward an experience that most intimately combines (biologically and psychologically) the self and another. This "other" is the germinating Word of God, which seems at first to grow in her as nourished by her body, but even as the God-man's life progresses, it becomes ever more clear that her own self and life are sustained by the Word of God. Mary's experience also reflects the surrender of her personal faith experience in the service of the church. Just as she must give up her son to his divine work to establish the church, Christians should not focus on personal experiences but on the realization that true faith exists in the service of the people of God.[8]

The incarnation is an affirmation of the human beyond anything any other human resource has to offer. In Christ, God reconciles humanity to himself, offering the peace and communion for which we were originally created. Here we find the conclusive answer to what it means to be fully human: to have abundant life through the restoration of our communion with the Maker of creation. Do you want to know who we are? We are God's children. This knowledge of ourselves, however, which should direct all our thoughts and actions, is pronounced within history and requires application to history in our present historical-cultural situation and in each particular vocation.

This means that our knowledge of God and hence our self-knowledge are crucially tied to God's self-revelation in the incarnation and its interpretation in the Bible as the word of God. God's

---

7. 2 Corinthians 5:16: "So from now on we regard no one from a worldly point of view." This viewpoint should not be distorted into meaning that we should only appreciate others as potential targets for evangelization but rather as intrinsically valuable, those for whom Christ has died, which may or may not result in their belief in God.

8. *Herrlichkeit*, 1:326–29.

self-revelation in Jesus the Christ does not, in other words, relieve us from the hard work of thinking and cosuffering with all of humanity. The Christian does not somehow stand above intellectual and cultural developments. The incarnation does, however, provide a definite goal for the humanistic concerns of self-knowledge and character formation. Critical reflection and worldview thinking informed by Christ's promise, are directed toward a peaceful, just society. The Christian is not called out of this world but into it, to reflect the new humanity Christ suggested in his earthly walk as suffering servant and healer.

Second, God's affirmation of human nature in the incarnation also points to the intrinsic worth of creation. Following the apostle Paul's Jewish notion that both humankind and nature look forward to final redemption, God's reconciliatory and restorative work includes the redemption of creation to its original goodness.[9] Creation and matter are themselves worthy of investigation because, by paying attention to them, we honor the Creator who is at work in them. Even though the actual design of the universe has turned out much more complex than science had imagined, science continues to operate on the basic assumption that the universe is somehow rationally designed in patterns that yield explanations for the empirical observations we make. If we abandon this notion, science itself becomes futile. If we embrace it, however, we have good grounds for interdisciplinary work. Created, fallen, and now reconciled to God through Christ's incarnation, death, and resurrection, all aspects of creation are gathered together in him toward the final redemption when "creation itself will be . . . brought into the glorious freedom of the children of God" (Romans 8:21). The dignity of nature is intrinsically bound up with the new humanity in Christ. For this reason, incarnational humanism views the various academic disciplines much as Paul views the church members: different parts united by serving one common Founder in the pursuit of humanity's restoration. In their different ways, the natural sciences, the humanities, and the arts pursue the same goal, albeit in different ways that should make use of the others' insights, methods, and conclusions.

In combination with human dignity, the intrinsic worth of nature also means that it has worth beyond functionality. A tree

9. Romans 8:18–24.

has worth beyond its value as timber, and a good education has value beyond the job market. The study of language, history, and ideas does not appear to be as useful as computer training, but because of the dignity of nature and human nature, they have intrinsic worth, and their patient study honors God's creation and thus glorifies God.

Third, the incarnation demonstrates that truth is always interpretation. If the fountain of all truth itself, God, does not exist for us in a vacuum but communicates himself to us linguistically and historically, all truth follows this pattern. The incarnation is God's word to humanity, God's self-interpretation in history. The historical manifestation of God in Jesus of Nazareth is the perfect exegesis of God, but its meaning depends on the cultural context in which it was uttered. As von Balthasar puts it: "Jesus Christ is the unique one, who is nonetheless interpretable only in the entire context of human history and the entire existing cosmos. He is the word and the picture, the expression and the exegesis of God through the entire human apparatus of historical existence between birth and death with all stages and conditions of life, using both individual and social structures."[10]

The incarnation does not allow for absolute truth as an abstract, timeless concept. Truth that transcends cultural limitations nonetheless arises from culture and is only communicable in language. In Jesus, God has fully expressed himself to us. This address is mediated through a certain historically determined culture with its social and linguistic conventions. Thus, God's truth comes to us through tradition. Not only does God use a particular people and time in history to reveal himself, the interpretation of the incarnation in the New Testament and subsequently by the church fathers and other commentators mediates this event and its meaning to us. We cannot circumvent this mediation by some miracle of the Holy Spirit that allows us direct, unmediated access to the mind of God; instead the Spirit works through the historico-linguistic means of the divine address—God's speaking to us—to convey truth.[11] This also means—and this is so for all truth—that knowledge of God

10. Hans Urs von Balthasar, *The Glory of the Lord*, vol. 1, *Seeing the Form* (San Francisco: Ignatius, 1998), 29.

11. The early church already relied on tradition, i.e., on the apostles' interpretation of Christ's life, death, and resurrection; see Acts 2:42. For apostolic authority in interpreting the gospel, see 1 Corinthians 7:17.

cannot be had without some kind of hard historical and exegetical work, interpreting either text or experience.[12]

We should not forget, however, that the incarnation also guards the transcendence of truth. By taking on fallen humanity and thus submitting to the flux of being in the world, God in no way compromises his total and complete otherness. And so the incarnation provides the solution for those thinkers who seek an unshakeable, irreducible norm for human dignity, but who dare not locate it firmly within this changeable world, in history and culture. This, you may recall, was precisely the fear of Levinas and his postmodern disciples of radical difference. For them, generalizing concepts or traditions tend to suppress opinions and voices that differ from the most dominant tradition. For them, the incarnation's claim that God takes on humanity seems impossible because, when God actually participates fully in the immanent world and its culture, God can no longer be greater than the world.[13] Yet the incarnation insists that God's enfleshment, God's mediation into culture in no way compromised God's total otherness. Incarnation offers us a model in which the totality of a cultural system of expression does not necessarily do away with difference. In the incarnation, God's self-expression, without any loss of transcendence, is mediated through language and culture. And so the stuff of this world is no longer a hindrance to God's self-communication by its true medium. The same goes for human dignity and human knowledge. Human nature and its truths are mediated through tradition and culture but are not reducible to them. Interpreting texts therefore does not necessarily mean subjectivism, the reduction of a truth to my culturally constructed interpretive grid, because truth, although incarnated in language and culture, also transcends its medium. In sum, the interpretation of a text or historical event, unless it is a willful distortion, is the very means by which truth reveals itself.

Moreover, according to this incarnational model of truth, not only is all truth interpretation; all interpretation also requires personal involvement and imagination. The notion of a disinter-

12. See, e.g., N. T. Wright, *The Challenge of Jesus* (Downers Grove, IL: InterVarsity, 1999).

13. Levinas, by contrast, would like to see the presence of God "pierce immanence without thereby taking one's place in it" ("A Man-God?" in *Entre nous* [New York: Columbia University Press, 1998], 55).

ested, neutral approach to truth is untenable first of all for the interpretation of God's word because to read it with the idea of neutrality is like reading a love letter with scientific objectivity. To read the Bible in this way is to reject its fundamental nature as personal address within the deeply human context of love and care. In fact, neutral exegesis of the biblical text is itself already a misreading. For example, to read the Scriptures with a neutral stance toward their central demand to recognize the lordship of Christ is already a misreading because it ignores the greater context and the reader's required relation to it, on which the meaning of the text depends.

This same principle, however, applies to all truth. No knowledge of anything is possible without personal involvement. This is all the truer in the humanities, where we study texts and records written by other human beings. There can be no question of indifferent exegesis (establishing what the text says neutrally) succeeded by personal application (what it means to me). Much like reading a love letter, understanding is possible only on the basis of personal interest. An objective assessment of what is true cannot be made without personal involvement with the material under investigation.

Common Ground: Incarnational Humanism and Secular Thinking

Given the saga of the university, the way humanism has turned on Christians, and the crisis of the contemporary university, you may well wonder how you can thrive during the years you spend there. If you attend a secular institution, you may think you will be lucky to complete a degree with your faith intact; if you attend a Christian one, you may worry that you have already marginalized yourself or, worse, may naively think that the most pressing academic issues of our time do not concern you. But do not throw in the towel or opt for a Christian bunker mentality.

On the contrary, since all truth is God's truth, you can learn in the environment of any contemporary university. You can connect on the issues that concern many people today. If you work hard, you can frame these issues in terms of Christian thought. To do so will both help you to appreciate the issues with which many people are struggling and enable you to set goals for your own education in these issues. The foundations of Christian theology are as relevant to the life of the mind today as they have ever been. Our engagement with postmodern thought in this book is meant to show that Christianity need not shy away from the current debates; it does not call you out of them to live in some never-never land.

At its best, Christian thought has demonstrated its ability to listen to various postmodern critiques of the modern condition, has perceived the signs of the times, and has developed new ways to engage the issues that are at once culturally sensitive and theologically appropriate. It is showing how trends in intellectual culture can be seen to be deeply consonant with theological doctrines properly understood.

Intellectual culture has come to recognize, first, that human nature is relational through and through; second, that we can still affirm a prominent role for human reason in spite of the abuses and limits of reason postmodernism has helped us to see; and third, that the world in which we live consists of signs in need of interpretation. Taken together, these three points affirm the complexity of what it means to be human and the centrality of this question. They suggest a coherence and common focus in intellectual pursuits that is at present undervalued and that Christian students can both affirm and take pleasure in exploring. These three points represent the common concern for our humanity that the Christian student will find in non-Christian institutions.

1. A human being is an agent, doing and thinking things in dynamic social reference—we think and do things in relation to other people. What do we mean when we say "I do this" or "I think that"? If we assume the word "individual" or "self" to mean that we are self-contained entities, we hide important aspects of reality from ourselves. If we think that we begin our contact with reality from a place of neutrality to which we retreat and from which we enter into negotiations with other human beings only when we want or need to, we will have a deficient understanding both of ourselves and of the reality with which we are inseparably related.

Over time, intellectuals have put an increasing emphasis on the individual. As so often is the case, the intention behind this development was good. In the pursuit of intellectual freedom, thinkers tried to loosen the bonds of authority structures and rigid traditions. The self, the thinking self, promised a refuge from warring religious and political agendas. Instead of beginning from history or from any supposed revelation outside ourselves, human consciousness became the starting point for all knowledge. It is understandable that thinkers tried to move away from the contingent, ever-changing, and thus unreliable realm of history and human relations into the sphere of the mind. Linked to universal reason, the self, reduced to the sphere of the thinking and reflecting mind, holds out the promise of agreement and unity, the place of eternal verities, where every conflict and difference is laid to rest.

The emphasis of Western thought on the isolated thinking mind as the essence of what it means to be human, however, is dehumanizing because it encourages isolation and hides from us our dependence on others. Paradoxically, while the model of the reflective mind strove toward independence and freedom, it in fact marooned us on the solipsistic island of the reflecting mind. In such a situation we are required to build a bridge to other islands. We suggest that the model is mistaken. While this view was in fact developed and embraced by Christian philosophers, it goes against the biblical portrayal of the human being as an agent in the world. It also goes against the more embodied and socially and culturally constituted conceptions of persons being developed in recent philosophy and cultural theory.

We are not individuals but persons. To be human is not to be a reflective consciousness but a person in relation. Reflection is important and necessary, but it is bound together with doing, and both of these function within social reference. We are persons in community with others rather than reflective islands. To be fully human is to embody and uphold laws that foster community and to strive for re-creative relationship with the natural environment.

2. Reason merits a strong but careful defense. To the extent that it has been defined in conjunction with the isolated thinking mind, it is in need of a thoroughgoing critique. As part of a more embodied conception of persons, however, there remains an important place for an emphasis on humanity's capacity for critical reflection. Reason's detractors have widely challenged it as being disembodied, artificially and wrongly separated from our emotions, or a mere pretense masking relationships based on power. Some of its would-be defenders exacerbate the situation

by making reason unassailable and betraying their anxious need for an utterly stable point of reference (in other words, treating it as an idol they entirely comprehend). Yet many thinkers in the history of thought, from Socrates onward, have engaged reason interactively rather than treat it as something brittle.

Within a more corporately embodied understanding of persons, reason should be understood as context-dependent and continually unfolding insight rather than utter and complete clarity. We never attain the latter. What we do attain is an unfolding sense of disclosure, a partial and provisional clarity that helps us to understand our situation, but without the confidence that we can make totalizing pronouncements as a result. Reason is our ability to reflect on our existence; reason, however, is not a mere intellectual activity that promises direct and pure access to complete truth—such is the privilege of God. But even God is not pure reason; God, particularly in the Judeo-Christian tradition, is relational through and through.

Reason is primarily the means by which we know that we do not know everything and the means by which we enjoy our world. It includes our emotions. It never stands alone and is not the cool center of our being apart from our emotions, apart from others or from the past. Rational reflection depends on personal motives and cultural and educational influences. Reason is not a set of ready-made assumptions about or interpretations of reality that somehow float unchangingly and eternally in the heavens, just waiting to be discovered.

Instead reason is our reflective ability and our rational interpretations of reality as shaped by the books we read, the people we grow up with, the culture we live in, the language(s) we speak, the things we do. To think rationally is already to think in dialogue with other human beings and with traditions that are older and greater than ourselves. Reason is not beholden to politics, and yet it is inescapably political. It is potentially universal, although its unfolding character means that we never have complete clarity as individuals or collectively. Toleration is always required. And humility. They always will be.

3. Reality, for humans, is textual. One of the most far-reaching conclusions in twentieth-century thought has been the idea that language shapes us in ways different from, and to an extent far greater than, most thinkers had hitherto imagined. For instance,

our ability to think is bound up with the terms we learn through our informal and formal education. The last century's appreciation of language also undermined individualism because we only acquire language in a social context. It also focused attention on the ubiquitous role of interpretation. Associated with translation and commentary, language helped twentieth-century thinkers come to appreciate the importance of interpretation as a fundamental human activity.

Some postmodern commentators pursued the implications of the shaping force of language to argue that we are imprisoned by language or that all meaning is completely relative, just as words have meaning only relative to one another. At one time books, for Renaissance humanism in particular, had symbolized a fount of life-giving and liberating knowledge; a book was something one opened up to discover things. In postmodern hands, the emphasis lay more on the page, with its combination of text and margin, its diacritical marks, its impenetrable and austere thinness. The term "textuality" came to draw one's attention to physical properties rather than subject matter because there was no stable meaning in the text.

What is a text? Hundreds of years ago it would have meant a precious manuscript, or a book off a newfangled printing press, or perhaps a letter. Now it can mean all of these things, or a DVD, or a commercial, or a bodily gesture, or a voice—any human expression that intentionally or unintentionally carries meaning. Just as reason is situated (not the cool, detached center of our being) in a cultural linguistic context, so also do texts participate in this context. In this way, nothing is outside text. The world in which we live can never be absolutely divided up into its material and immaterial elements, neither linguistic and nonlinguistic nor cultural and natural. Rather, these realms are always inseparably intertwined.

Much like the tradition of humanism, we believe that texts help us develop our ability to think, enable communication with others, and contribute to the ethical life by providing moral instruction and examples (including examples of complexity and moral ambiguity). In our current climate, the emphasis on politics encourages the healthy suspicion that texts may serve as vehicles for political power. Unfortunately, some have concluded that this is all texts do, encouraged by a dim view of finding a stable meaning in a text.

Textuality, including an emphasis on language and interpretation, does not entail complete arbitrariness in the quest for meaning. Competence in reading and writing is necessary to reconstruct the dominant interpretation of a text. Contrary to popular perception, one of the founding figures of postmodernity has always upheld this view: "Otherwise, one could indeed say just anything at all and I have never accepted saying, or being encouraged to say, just anything at all."[14] While not relativistic, a proper view of textuality does entail the recognition of our limitations as creatures. As finite human beings, we do not have access to complete clarity in interpretation.

Conclusion

The incarnation makes possible a humanism that acknowledges the important postmodern criticisms of modernity we have examined so far but also avoids the cul-de-sac of meaningless fragmentation. Dominant strains of postmodernism focused so strongly on difference and particularity that they could no longer assert any commonality in answering the most important question: what does it mean to be fully human?

Postmodernism rejects any overarching narrative that would allow for a determinate answer to this question, because of the belief that such solutions are a thinly veiled grasp for power and domination. In this wholesale rejection of overarching narratives, postmodernism has overlooked the one grand narrative that is able to present a solution to Enlightenment dualism and yet resist any one story's grasp for power. In the incarnation we encounter a model of truth that is both interpretive and yet assertive. Hence, none of the postmodern criticisms against any universally valid truth claim really apply in this case. Christian revelation is not a disguised grasp for power. First of all, it is not disguised, since it announces clearly God's lordship over all things. Second, the practical communal bond with this sovereign God is purchased through sacrifice rather than conquest, by giving one's life for another, which is also the basis of the community inspired by this religion.

14. Jacques Derrida, quoted in Simon Critchley, *The Ethics of Deconstruction: Derrida and Levinas*, 2nd ed. (West Lafayette, IN: Purdue University Press, 1999), 24.

It is unfortunate that postmodernity, in its turn against secular scientific humanism, has still clung tenaciously to one of the main driving forces of that humanism—that Christianity is a large part of the problem. Although it is true that historically Christianity has identified itself wrongly with dehumanizing ideas and practices, Christianity alone contains the remedy for these very aberrations. The postmodern criticism ends at deconstruction, whereas incarnational humanism offers the real potential for recovering the great themes of humanism outlined in this book under the twin aspects of the dignity of nature and the dignity of the human. The incarnation affirms the intrinsic worth of nature and thus immediately checks creation's reduction to resource material. It also validates all research into every aspect of God's work, whether in the natural sciences or in the humanities.

The incarnation presents us with another definite purpose of university education: to proclaim and celebrate the affirmation of the human and of nature that is offered in the life, death, and resurrection of Jesus Christ. This is merely a more focused way to express the greatest commandment, to love God with all our heart, strength, mind, and soul. We do not want to launch into yet another tirade on how Christians have neglected the mind in their witness. It is, however, crucially important that Christians realize the nature of this witness. The incarnation offers self-knowledge in light of God's revelation—scholarship and knowledge in the service of God's redemptive purposes for a new earth and humanity restored to the trinitarian image. We are social beings destined for communal living in righteousness, justice, and unity, and the method for promoting these kingdom values that frame all knowledge is suffering rather than conquest. In this way, the first great commandment flows naturally into the second: love your neighbor as yourself.

Incarnational humanism, however, also means that such self-knowledge cannot be had in the abstract but must be acquired through suffering in the broadest sense. In an earlier chapter, Vico talked about the discipline required for higher education, and you will find his predictions to be true: the best students are self-disciplined students. This virtue helps considerably in your later professional life. Incarnational humanism, however, also means that our proclamation of who we are according to God's restored humanity in Christ is continually evolving. Thus, as cultural paradigms of our human nature change, the serious Christian student will acquire anew what it means to be fully human. For many people, it is very difficult to understand and grasp the current cultural upheaval from modernity to postmodernity and beyond. The Christian student does not stand above these changes but, true to the incarnational model, lives in the midst of them, experiences them, and wrestles with them.

In understanding these issues properly, the Christian student is affirming the incarnation, one's own and others' humanity. After all, if the New Testament is right, Christ did not come to pluck souls from an evil and worthless creation and transport them to an angelic existence; instead he came to announce the beginning of the world's renewal. What does this mean to you, a student currently engaged in the task of scholarship? All Christians, of course, are "called to knowledge of God, themselves, of one another, of the world"[15] and to be renewed in knowledge after the image of the Creator.[16] As a student, however, your particular calling is the task of scholarship. The quality, character, and direction of your scholarly pursuits are a witness to God and participate in God's new creation. By pursuing knowledge, you engage in the diligent study of nature and human nature for the sake of the kingdom and its restorative, redemptive work.

Once you realize that spirituality and learning are not separate but deeply connected, so that cultural trends may either confirm or contradict the true humanity announced and embodied in Jesus, you realize how hard and yet how rewarding real thinking in the service of the kingdom becomes. Love of wisdom now means that you have to learn the cultural context of the biblical message concerning who we are. At the same time, you must reflect on how your particular Christian faith may have distorted this message by buying into unbiblical cultural ideas and also analyze contemporary culture and its direction in light of the Scriptures. No doubt, this is difficult work, but the Christian is called to nothing less: "You are called to be truly human, but it is nothing short of the life of God within you that enables you to be so, to

15. Wright, *Challenge*, 194.
16. Colossians 3:10. Paul speaks here about the new self, "which is being renewed in knowledge in the image of its Creator."

be remade in God's image."[17] Incarnational humanism advocates this inseparable cohesion between intellect and faith; it is a faith that seeks understanding in the service of God's kingdom and for the benefit of all.

What does this activity look like in the daily grind of university life? To move from theory to a more practical look at scholarship in the service of humanism, we now turn to the notion of common grace, the idea that God's incarnation enables you to roll up your sleeves and explore knowledge not only without fear but also in confidence that in God's providence non-Christian minds have provided many great ideas that contribute to our renewed humanity.

Study Questions

1. Given what you have read so far, do you think Jesus is a humanist?
2. What three central humanistic elements does the incarnation affirm? How?
3. To what extent does the incarnation allow for convergence with current secular academic concern for the categories of agency, rationality, and textuality?

17. Wright, *Challenge*, 193.

APPLYING
INCARNATIONAL
HUMANISM

11

INCARNATIONAL HUMANISM
AND COMMON GRACE

"What have the Romans ever done for us?!"
Reg, a zealot in *Life of Brian*
(aka John Cleese)

CHRIST'S INCARNATION MEANS THE END of dualism. In becoming flesh, God affirms humanity and creation as such, and Christians should be servants of God's general grace for the benefit of all humanity. Incarnational humanism affirms this teaching but, in applying it to university studies, also insists on the humble acceptance of God's presence in non-Christian achievements. Common grace is a two-way street, and our full understanding of this issue will allow us not only to tolerate non-Christian contributions to knowledge but actually to seek truth in them that contributes to the renewal of our minds. We are not merely agents but also grateful recipients of common grace. As

167

an illustration of what this means academically, we will look at the work of the Christian scholar C. S. Lewis.

L⟩ woot woot¡

Introduction

In an influential book entitled *How Now Shall We Live?* former Nixon aide and Christian convert Chuck Colson recognizes dualism as a problem that requires the incarnation as the solution. For Colson—and we would ardently agree—many Christians practice dualism these days. They do so by keeping their faith private, separate from the big, mostly bad world out there, the world of politics, culture, and the workplace. If we concentrate solely on prayer, Bible study, and Christian fellowship and are not trying to influence our culture for Christ in practical, hands-on ways, then we are living in a Christian bubble. We are living dualistically, still under the influence of the Enlightenment's creed "that religion and society are split off from each other. Religion is what people do with their solitude."[1]

Such dualism, whose development in university culture we have traced from the Middle Ages to the Enlightenment and beyond, represents an extremely important challenge. Christians and non-Christians alike need to get over the tendency to separate religion from the rest of society. Our thinking in matters of religion is part of our entire worldview, and our religion can and ought to be brought to bear on our politics and cultural practices. Just as God affirmed human culture through the incarnation, we want to encourage you not to avoid the wider culture but fearlessly and critically to explore this common ground on which Christians and non-Christians can and do cooperate. We have seen that the incarnation, God's expressing himself in culture even while transcending it, provides the foundation for this confidence.

For many Christians, this connection means that Christians should work hard to become active shapers of culture, to influence society with explicitly Christian ideas and practices. Colson expresses this idea by insisting that Christians should see themselves

---

1. N. T. Wright, *Bringing the Church to the World* (Minneapolis: Bethany House, 1992), 20.

as *agents* of common grace.[2] Common grace is the means by which God sustains his creation and restrains evil; agents of common grace are people who help God dispense his general favor to humanity and the world. Colson would have us overcome dualism and burst out of our Christian bubbles by recognizing that God means for his people to help transform God's world by promoting Christian values beyond the limits of the holy huddle. This entails getting involved in politics, protecting the environment, and so on. So far, so good—we need to see ourselves as agents of God's grace in the world.[3] But do only Christians do these things? Are Christians the only agents of common grace?

Colson's emphasis on the role of Christians is striking in what it leaves out. He writes as if Christians were the main positive contributors to culture. Colson's one-sided interpretation of common grace falls short of the classical understanding of this notion in the Christian tradition.

Christians as Recipients of Common Grace

We want to return to a fuller notion of common grace by establishing the presence of God's sustaining grace in *every* aspect of creation, including the intellect. To put the question of common grace in a broad context: we must ask about the ability of human reason to establish truth in a fallen world. What are the effects of sin on the mind, and to what extent does a Christian have a superior insight into truth?

Our concept of common grace is basically a defense of human reason as the gift of God given to all. But is not reason itself impaired by sin? This question has enjoyed a long standing debate in church history, with many subtle turns and twists that cannot

2. Chuck Colson and Nancy Pearcey, *How Now Shall We Live?* (Wheaton, IL: Tyndale House, 1999), xii.

3. As Christians, we bear the fragrance of Christ. We cannot help but be a blessing to others around us, and we need to realize that we have a responsibility to be so. We need to be intentional about using our God-given talents for the service of others. This means taking our high regard for justice into energetic approaches to law and politics, embodying the love of Christ in our commitment to social reform and the medical professions, using our disciplined personal habits to achieve breakthroughs in research, and compelling expression of our culture's identity and desires in the arts and athletics.

possibly be reproduced for you here. Generally, however, all orthodox parties in this debate agree on this: reason is a gift from God
and as such is dependent on God's sustaining grace. Theologians
speak here of the doctrine of illumination, which says that our
mental activity is possible only because God constantly illumines
our minds. Thomas Aquinas, for example, states that "we must
therefore say that, if a man is to know any truth whatsoever, he
needs divine help in order that his intellect may be moved to its
act by God."[4]

Because of this natural light that God dispenses freely to every
intellect, even the mind marred by the effects of sin is able to discern
truths. Clearly, Aquinas had a bigger view of God's activity than
many hold today. Every truth rightly discerned by any human being
is an act of common divine grace; we "always need divine help for
any thinking, in so far as God moves the intellect to act."[5]

Theologians such as Aquinas did make a clear distinction, however, between natural and supernatural insights. Although the
unregenerate mind could very well discern (assisted always by
God's grace) truths concerning nature or even truths concerning
our general human nature, it could not discern things that went
beyond this natural order. Although God's Spirit operates indeed
on every mind that thinks, there is a special operation of the Spirit.
The mind, says Aquinas, "cannot know intelligible things of a
higher order unless it is perfected by a stronger light, such as the
light of faith or prophecy, which is called 'the light of glory.'"[6] So,
first, we must affirm that the non-Christian can know as much
as—and often, by God's grace, more than—the Christian concerning nature and human nature. There is a difference in knowledge,
however, when it comes to knowing God as God revealed himself
in Christ. This knowledge is a gift from God in addition to God's
common grace and is reserved for the Christian.

Yet there remains this problem: we claim, on the one hand, that
the non-Christian mind can discern truth as well as the next person
except for the knowledge of God. Yet we have also claimed that
the knowledge of God is quintessential for our self-knowledge, for

4. Thomas Aquinas, *Summa theologica* Ia-IIae, q. 109, art. 1, in *Nature and Grace,*
139.
5. Ibid.
6. Ibid.

our understanding of what it means to be human. Do we not claim, then, that the Christian mind is in fact by definition superior to the non-Christian mind? Do we not postulate another form of dualism here by opposing Christian rationality to a non-Christian variant? The answer lies in delineating carefully the exact effects of sin on the mind. We turn again to Aquinas: "A man cannot even know truth without divine help. Now his nature is impaired by sin more in the desire for good than in the knowledge of truth."[7] What Aquinas means is that all truth is God's truth but our integration of true insights into our greater life context marks the difference between the Christian and the non-Christian. Christians, not on their own initiative but on account of God's drawing them into communion with him, will see all knowledge within the context of God's love. The difference, in other words, lies in the use of truth rather than in its sheer recognition.

Similarly, John Calvin defined the inability of the fallen mind to see reality in the context of God's love as the corruption of the entire person, including the mind: "Calvin did not think of corruption as affecting the being of the mind itself, for the mind is still maintained in being by the direct action of God. As a natural gift it is not removed but perverted."[8] Contrary to Enlightenment thinkers, Calvin did not separate the mind from the rest of the person. For Calvin, the mind has not lost its ability to think per se, but it has lost its proper framework for applying its insights; reason has lost its God-directed coordinate. Reason, as he put it, is corrupted "as far as its rectitude is concerned."[9] Thus, from a Christian perspective, the disadvantage of the non-Christian is twofold. First, the unbeliever cannot know things about God that are hidden in Christ and are known only in relation with God. Second, the non-Christian lacks the believer's context for reason, the recognition that all things are for the glory of God. The non-Christian thus lacks "the knowledge of God and His will, and the means of framing the life in accordance with them."[10]

So, when we claim that reason is affected by sin, we have to understand this influence precisely: the mind itself and its Chris-

7. Thomas Aquinas, *Summa theologica* Ia-IIae, q. 109, art. 2, in *Nature and Grace*, 141.

8. T. F. Torrance, *Calvin's Doctrine of Man* (London: Lutterworth, 1952), 118.

9. Calvin, *Institutes*, quoted ibid., 119.

10. Calvin, *Institutes* 2.2.13.

tian and non-Christian achievements alike are a glorious testimony to God's gift of reason. Non-Christian insights are "wrong" only insofar as they miss the context in which all knowledge gains its full measure, namely, when it is dedicated and used for the glory of God.

Intellectual achievements are not, in other words, the exclusive domain of the Christian. And so Calvin insists that we should learn from non-Christians in "physics, dialectics, mathematics, and other similar science . . . [lest] we be justly punished for our laziness."[11]

In short, the effects of sin on reason do not at all hinder us from respecting and celebrating the astonishing abilities of the human mind, wherever we find them manifest, as the gift of God to humanity. Calvin taught that "we see among all mankind that reason is proper to our nature. . . . Now, because some are born fools or stupid, that defect does not obscure the general grace of God. . . . Some men excel in keenness, others are superior in judgment; still others have a readier wit to learn this or that art. In this variety God commends his grace to us, lest anyone should claim as his own what flowed from the sheer bounty of God."[12] Calvin held that human greatness in the arts and sciences is a natural proof of God's grace, which blesses Christians and non-Christians alike. Another way of saying this is that you do not have to be a Christian to be smart. And, incidentally, being a Christian does not guarantee a keen intellect. Colson emphasizes the contribution of Christians, yet in God's providence human society benefits greatly from the non-Christian also.

In the context of university education, Christians need first to recognize all that they have in common with non-Christians. Through the university, Christians have often been *recipients* of common grace—of ideas and practices that arise through teaching and research that make everyone's life better. What is more, this grace regularly comes to people through non-Christians. Let us not be shy about the real situation: in such a context as ours, Christians can and do benefit enormously from the work done by their non-Christian counterparts.

To take just one example, Christians, along with everyone else, benefit massively from the advances in Western medicine. Much

11. Calvin, *Institutes* 2.2.16.
12. Calvin, *Institutes* 1.2.17.

of the money, energy, and confidence placed in the development of medical technology is based on a modern secular scientific worldview. Christians need to acknowledge that buying into this worldview has not been without its benefits. Surely no one wants to argue that he or she would be as happy in an eighteenth-century hospital as a modern one. Faced with how the odds of beating certain forms of cancer have gone up dramatically in the last thirty years, surely one would hesitate to call the single-minded commitment to beating cancer excessive, misguided, or a sign of humanistic hubris.

The secular scientific worldview has provided a framework that has produced impressive results. If all truth is God's truth, this is not surprising. Common ground means that cooperation in vast areas of daily life is possible even if we espouse different worldviews.

Western culture has benefited immeasurably from the work of people on whom Christians (or a portion of the church, at least) took a dim view; and even many of those who have opposed Christianity, such as Nietzsche, have spoken with a prophetic power that helps to break the bonds of cultural habits of thinking that may be less than Christian or decidedly unbiblical but in which Christians often become bound, just like everyone else. The outstanding influence of different Christian figures and movements in history, such as William Wilberforce in bringing down the institution of slavery in Britain or Mother Theresa in bringing relief to the streets of Calcutta, is undeniable. But as we have seen in the development of the university, Christians have not been immune to dualism or to other forms of sub-Christian thinking.

Part of our defense of postmodernism is on these grounds. It is not only—maybe not even primarily—Christians who have drawn attention to the negative implications of Enlightenment and modernist habits of thinking. Although Christians may be well positioned to point out how modern developments are dualistic (rightly seeing parallels with battles the early church had to fight), others have sometimes shown the way.

Christians need to acknowledge the positive and fruitful contributions of all kinds of intellectuals throughout history, which are blessings in and of themselves for society, for the church, and for individuals right down to the level of character formation. A good Christian scholar who takes the implications of incarnational humanism seriously will thus look for the beneficial aspects in other worldviews before judging them. The positive aspects of the Enlightenment are a case in point: it may have made a god out of reason, but there are usually good reasons people are seduced by gods the way they are. To list only two of the Enlightenment's benefits again: its naturalism allowed people to concentrate their minds on unlocking some of the secrets of nature, and in the field of politics and political theory, Enlightenment liberalism contributed to the increased value placed on basic human rights and liberties. The situation the Christian student faces is a little like the scene in the Monty Python movie _Life of Brian_, when the zealot leader Reg asks rhetorically, "What have the Romans ever done for us?!" The others take the question at face value and the answers trickle in: roads, education, aqueducts . . . quite a lot when they thought about it. So it is with the secular humanism of the Enlightenment, and so it is with many elements of postmodern thought. Christians look silly when they dismiss these resources.

On the good in non-Christian intellectual life, explicit Christian commentary is surprisingly limited and evasive. Perhaps Christians think that the point goes without saying: of course, everyone benefits from advances made by all kinds of people all over the world, and no Christian would be so arrogant as to claim that only Christians make beneficial discoveries. Surely this is why most Christian commentators insist on universal access to reason—they want to celebrate and to promote the shared nature of our learning. Don't they?

It is interesting that Christian assaults on various cultural conditions, from humanism to postmodernism, baldly identify their opponents as Marxists, Freudians, naturalists, feminists, and so on. Yet when it comes to talking about benefits from the surrounding culture, Christians regularly praise faceless reason, as if reason were not embedded in concrete contributions by real human beings. Christians could and should be much more gracious about acknowledging the contributions of others and the ideological contexts out of which these insights arise. This understanding of common grace is vital for your understanding of university education. To illustrate this importance, this chapter ends by showcasing an academic whose work demonstrates an exemplary grasp of common grace's benefits for Christian scholarship, the British intellectual and Christian apologist C. S. Lewis.

C. S. Lewis on Tradition and the Intellectual Life

Amazingly, Christians regularly fail to acknowledge the dimension of common grace in the thought of the most revered modern saint in Protestant hagiography, C. S. Lewis (1898–1963). Two important tenets of Lewis's system of apologetics—his celebration of reason and his understanding of tradition—show how a generous understanding of common grace undergirds his writings. The inherent attractiveness of Lewis's work as an apologist rests on his affirmation of common ground between Christians and non-Christians. His worldview minimizes the divide separating Christianity and secular culture.

Although many Christians enlist Lewis for his arguments and rhetoric, it is much more challenging to appropriate the presuppositions that inform his approach. There is no shortage of proof-texting from Lewis, but the undergirding philosophy of common grace remains obscure. In this vein, Colson cites Lewis as a major influence yet makes no mention of Christians as recipients as well as agents of common grace. Though popular as an apologetic weapon, upon closer study Lewis undermines an ethos of the opposition, or belief in the strict incompatibility, of worldviews.

Lewis's recognition of reason as the common ground of all human expression grounds his understanding of common grace. His celebration of reason is straightforward enough. It gives his famous *Screwtape Letters* their initial force and energy. In the very first letter that the senior devil Screwtape sends to his nephew Wormwood about keeping people from becoming Christians, he warns him about the dangers of rational argument:

> The trouble about argument is that it moves the whole struggle onto the Enemy's own ground. He can argue too; whereas in really practical propaganda of the kind I am suggesting, He has been shown for centuries to be greatly the inferior of Our Father Below. By the very act of arguing, you awake the patient's reason, and once it is awake, who can foresee the result?[13]

For Lewis, reason levels the playing field, and because God has constructed his universe along rational principles, once reason is awakened, it can lead one to God. In Lewis, God's gift of reason

13. C. S. Lewis, *The Screwtape Letters* (New York: Macmillan, 1943), 12.

affirms the Enlightenment principle of *Sapere aude!* Daring to think shifts the battle to the Enemy's (i.e., God's) ground. For Screwtape, even though it may be possible to divert a human's rational processes, awakening reason is dangerous. And so he does not like the sciences. The logical rigor demanded in the sciences makes them dangerous from a devilish point of view: "Above all, do not attempt to use science (I mean, the real sciences) as a defence against Christianity. They will positively encourage him to think about realities he can't touch and see."[14] Although Lewis is fully aware of the limitations of a naturalistic worldview, he appreciates the commitment to rationality in the sciences.

Yet Lewis also warns his readers not to separate reason from religion. In his space trilogy, for example, Lewis challenges the hubris of science by exploring the place of rationality in various academic disciplines. He suggests that science needs the guidance of governing principles. Lewis does not suspect reason, but he does suspect some scientists of an inability to acknowledge the limitations of their own rational abilities and of the presence in their lives of other motivating factors.

Although Lewis criticizes our natural tendency to justify our particular desires and scholarly goals with an appeal to the neutrality of reason, he insists on the importance of clear, rational thought. To surrender reason is to become enslaved by its opposite, propaganda and muddled thinking. In the third part of the trilogy, *That Hideous Strength*, Lewis focuses on a young sociologist, whom he describes as "a man of straw": "His education had been neither scientific nor classical—merely 'Modern.' The severities both of abstraction and of high human tradition had passed him by: and he had neither peasant shrewdness nor aristocratic honour to help him. He was a man of straw, a glib examinee in subjects that require no exact knowledge."[15] Quite apart from this being a scathing indictment of a system of education that is still with us, Lewis here again emphasizes the severity of abstraction, or reason, and laments the passing of the requirement of "exact knowledge."

At the same time, however, Lewis acknowledges that knowledge never comes to us unmediated but is passed down to us in the

14. Ibid., 14.
15. C. S. Lewis, *That Hideous Strength* (London: Pan, 1955), 109. This edition is an abridgment by the author of the story first published in 1945.

form of tradition. Focusing on reason alone results in a hopeless divide between modern Lewis-inspired apologetics and postmodernism. Too many devotees of Lewis appeal to his apologetics with just such a rationalistic agenda. One needs to supplement reason, as Lewis himself did. Lewis is quite unlike a modernist in holding reason together with tradition. As we have noted, for many "modern" Christians, as for many Enlightenment skeptics, tradition implies a blind adherence to the past. Many Protestant evangelicals think of the Reformation as the toppling of tradition and authority in favor of personal reason, the former embodied in the Catholic hierarchy, the latter evident in the picture of an individual reading the Bible for her- or himself.

Lewis, however, obviously thinks of tradition positively. It is the common ground which Christians and non-Christians share and upon which all develop their viewpoints. He puts a classical education on the same footing as a scientific one and treats "high human tradition" as equally valid as "abstraction." Both require exact knowledge and differ markedly from modern disciplines. Lewis values a high human tradition, a body of knowledge that all humans can share. The rationality of science is accessible to all, and so too is the learning he calls tradition. This perspective heightens the value of the humanities and of humanism in his apologetics.

A full appreciation of his approach to the relationship between Christians and the surrounding culture depends in part on recognizing how broadly he applies logic and what he includes as worthy of study: classical languages; the stories of ancient cultures; the history, laws, and beliefs of different and ancient peoples. All these can contribute to our understanding of tradition, and through them we obtain self-knowledge, that is, an orientation in our present cultural situation in comparison to the development of ideas concerning the ideal forms of human existence throughout the ages.

None of this may seem too terribly alarming to Christians who want to see education return to the cozy humanistic values of a liberal arts education, as if this were identical with a Christian education. Lewis's point, however, is rather different. Even in their zeal to renew their minds in Christ, Christians share a large pool of knowledge with non-Christians. This point comes across very clearly in Lewis's argument that there is no such thing as Christian ethics. Far from believing that Christianity ushers in a peculiar set of commands, he argues that such Christian doctrines as the atonement and the offer of forgiveness for sins indicate a moral law already recognized and known to have been broken:

> The idea (at least in its grossest and most popular form) that Christianity brought a new ethical code into the world is a grave error. If it had done so, then we should have to conclude that all who first preached it wholly misunderstood their own message: for all of them, its Founder, His precursor, His apostles, came demanding repentance and offering forgiveness, a demand and an offer both meaningless except on the assumption of a moral law already known and already broken.[16]

The idea of a shared awareness of the human condition is powerfully reinforced by the verses immediately following the famous John 3:16. God does not send his Son to create a problem (i.e., to condemn the world) but rather to fix an already existing one (our awareness that we already stand condemned because we know that we have broken the moral law).

In *The Abolition of Man*, Lewis refers to this shared great tradition of a natural moral law as the Tao. The doctrine of the Tao is the same in a variety of different forms, Platonic, Aristotelian, Stoic, Jewish, Christian, Oriental: "It is the doctrine of objective value, the belief that certain attitudes are really true, and others really false, to the kind of thing the universe is and the kind of things we are."[17] Lewis's conception of tradition overlaps with his commitment to rationality: both indicate a belief in something universally accessible. More explicitly than rationality, the Tao challenges commonly voiced assumptions about the uniqueness of Christians as God's agents of common grace. One can find in many different cultures the kind of moral commitment that provides the energy for those cultures to strive to make intellectual advances, to improve the lot of all kinds of people, and to order shared human life with respect for the past as well.

16. C. S. Lewis, "On Ethics," in *Christian Reflections*, ed. Walter Hooper (Grand Rapids: Eerdmans, 1967), 46.
17. C. S. Lewis, *The Abolition of Man* (1943) (London: Fount, 1999), 12.

If humanity shares a great tradition, then it is just possible that different cultures, and people with different perspectives, will be in positions to remind others of details being forgotten. Perhaps it is not possible for one group to bear everything in mind from the Tao and apply it to the present situation. Such a recognition of a group's limitations opens up the possibilities of receiving grace through other perspectives. It may be the case that Christianity, understood as the sum totality of all its manifestations in all times and places, represents the fullness of God's grace in Christ, but each cultural manifestation of Christianity, of the church, be it the crusading Christendom of the Middle Ages or twentieth-century evangelical Protestants, suffers from ideological limitations that the Holy Spirit will transcend only with the culmination of history in the second coming.

Lewis's emphasis on common grace has been echoed recently by Charles Taylor, who is both a believer and an eminent moral philosopher. Taylor candidly admits that we simply would not have some of the most cherished institutions in our modern world without the influence of non-Christian thinkers and cultural forces:

> The view I'd like to defend, if I can put it in a nutshell, is that in modern, secularist culture there are mingled together both authentic developments of the gospel, of an incarnational mode of life, and also a closing off to God that negates the gospel. The notion is that modern culture, in breaking with the structures and beliefs of Christendom, also carried certain facets of Christian life further than they ever were taken or could have been taken within Christendom.[18]

Perhaps Christians tend to focus on the skepticism of non-Christians and to see them as opponents. Yet people who explicitly reject Christianity can nonetheless be deeply humane, and to the extent that they defend the good in human beings, their achievements can ultimately be deeply Christian. This is what Taylor means when he suggests that secularist culture offers "authentic developments of the gospel, of an incarnational mode of life." At the same time, non-Christians will inevitably negate the gospel in some ways. There is no question of taking on board modern secularity wholesale,

18. Charles Taylor, *A Catholic Modernity?* (New York: Oxford University Press, 1999), 16.

but neither is an affirmation of society's indebtedness to secular achievements a slippery slope. One needs discernment.[19]

Such a broadened recognition of common grace does not recommend itself to those interested in quick fixes or the straightforward application of a body of knowledge already conceived in advance to be the whole truth. This outlook situates human learning in the midst of an existing, shared set of references. In terms of ethics, which is a dimension to be included whenever one considers the value or the purpose of education (as Levinas reminds us), problems constantly arise that should alert the educator to the limitations of his or her perspective. Lewis believes that neither Christians nor non-Christians should cut themselves off from the sources we all hold in common as we grope for solutions to improve human society.

For Lewis, God has deposited in human tradition the means that illumine our understanding of the same goal Jesus had: the healing and restoration of humanity. The difference between Christianity and the great tradition lies in the means of achieving this goal, not in the goal itself. Those who want to abandon morality altogether have cut themselves off from humanity already; those, however, who concern themselves with the fate of human society are already participants in God's common grace. God does not simply tell us step-by-step how to implement just laws but requires the interpretive application of tradition to our present cultural situation. Lewis presents to Christians and non-Christians alike this difficult and risky demand on our thinking:

19. We can look at Taylor's insight from the other side of the coin also. Some of the ideas of well-intentioned Christian apologists have had negative effects over the long haul. The plight of modernity is most commonly blamed on one man in particular, René Descartes. It is an oversimplification to blame the development of Western thought on one individual, and most would carefully qualify such a statement, but Descartes nevertheless appears prominently in the usual lists of suspects for our decline, especially where this decline is characterized by excessive fragmentation and individualism. There is good reason for the accusation. Descartes gave us the famous saying "I think, therefore I am." Ultimately, he put far too much emphasis on the subject (the I) and the belief that we could achieve real certainty without reference to God. His intention, however, was deeply Christian. If one reads the opening pages of his *Meditations on First Philosophy*, one is struck by his commitment to belief in God and the soul as laid down by Holy Scripture, and his laudable desire to present biblical truth in ways acceptable to philosophers rather than theologians. Unfortunately, his intentions were overtaken by the unforeseen consequence of negating certain aspects of the gospel, particularly those concerning the relationality of both God and humans.

The man without a moral code, like the animal, is free from moral problems. The man who has not learned to count is free from mathematical problems. A man asleep is free from all problems. Within the framework of general human ethics problems will, of course, arise and will sometimes be solved wrongly. This possibility of error is simply the symptom that we are awake, not asleep, that we are men, not beasts or gods. If I were pressing on you a panacea, if I were recommending traditional ethics as a means to some end, I might be tempted to promise you the infallibility which I actually deny. But that, you see, is not my position. I send you back to your nurse and your father, to all the poets and sages and law givers, because, in a sense, I hold that you are already there whether you recognize it or not: that there is really no ethical alternative: that those who urge us to adopt new moralities are only offering us the mutilated or expurgated text of a book which we already possess in the original manuscript.[20]

Lewis implies that a good education necessarily includes an ethical dimension. Furthermore, he argues that this education can draw on a common background that it must apply by interpreting the meaning of this tradition for specific cultural situations. By cutting itself off from tradition, the Enlightenment helped to precipitate the current educational crisis. Tradition does not simply solve our problems, as the Enlightenment saw. But for Lewis, that is all right. Humans make mistakes, not least in ethical matters. He simply wants us to acknowledge that we have collective wisdom at our disposal and that we need to deepen our familiarity with and reliance upon this tradition. Christians can make an excellent contribution in such a framework. They dare not presume, however, to isolate themselves as the only agents of common grace, as if they had a monopoly on truth.

The Christian missionary and cultural commentator Lesslie Newbigin (1909–1998) expresses a view of common grace similar to Lewis's. Newbigin forthrightly acknowledges shared common ground between people of different faiths, which he describes in terms of a shared story, the story of human existence:

The human story is one which we share with all other human beings—past, present, and to come. We cannot opt out of the story. We cannot take control of the story. It is under the control of the

20. Lewis, "On Ethics," 56.

infinitely patient God and Father of our Lord Jesus Christ. Every day of our lives we have to make decisions about the part we will play in the story, decisions which we cannot take without regard to the others who share the story. They may be Christians, Muslims, Hindus, secular humanists, Marxists, or of some other persuasion. They will have different understandings of the meaning and end of the story, but along the way there will be many issues in which we can agree about what should be done. There are struggles for justice and for freedom in which we can and should join hands with those of other faiths and ideologies to achieve specific goals, even though we know that the ultimate goal is Christ and his coming in glory and not what our collaborators imagine.[21]

Newbigin emphasizes the sense of common purpose that people of different faiths, or none, can share over "what should be done," even if they differ on their understanding of the meaning or end of the story of human existence. Such an attitude frees the Christian university student to immerse her- or himself in the issues of the day. It is, of course, important to have a sense of the overarching story, and the purpose of this book is to remind Christian students of this story, that is, the story of God's becoming human in Jesus Christ for the salvation of the world; yet students can and indeed must learn from others who do not share their understanding of the whole story.

Conclusion

We Christians would do well to recognize that we are also *recipients* of common grace at the hands of people of other faiths or of no faith at all. That we do not is perhaps one of the reasons non-Christians accuse us of arrogance: it appears that we do not like to admit just how much we have in common with them and how much we are indebted to them.

One of the ways Christians foster the impression of arrogance and shy away from the rich complexity of common grace is their insistence on reframing the terms of reference of intellectual discussion. It often seems that Christians want to ask metaphysical

21. Lesslie Newbigin, *The Gospel in a Pluralist Society* (Grand Rapids: Eerdmans, 1989), 181.

and salvific questions. One aspect of celebrating common grace is to appreciate life's vicissitudes and the finitude of our perspectives. Although Christians have faith that history has a goal and that "all will be well and all manner of things will be well," as a medieval mystic put it, we cannot know and cannot dwell in a future of which we have only fleeting knowledge. Although the incarnation has indeed ushered in a new age and God's inbreaking kingdom marks the beginning of the end of the present cosmic order, Christ came not to abandon humanity but to affirm and transform it.

If Christians were to commit themselves solely to the narrow task of saving souls, we might conclude that we ought to devote ourselves solely to prayer and fasting, fellowship, preaching, and missionary work. But then we have landed ourselves back in the problem of dualism. When Christians tacitly devalue life in this world by emphasizing salvation and ultimate purpose, such an attitude can easily come across as arrogance, as turning one's nose up at human existence.[22] Worldview thinking can itself encourage such an attitude of detachment. It can seduce one into pursuing an illusory point of reflective neutrality. Moreover, preoccupation with worldview can amount to an ongoing effort to reflect upon and to evaluate one's life rather than to live it. One can look too much for purpose and meaning.

If we do not want to go down this route, then we begin to see that, however important the questions of our ultimate purpose and destiny are, we all need to live in the here and now as well. With such a mind-set, we would do well to appreciate the achievements, the questions, and the perspectives—in short, the lives—of people in the here and now with whom we share a common story. Such an existential, incarnational dwelling in the world can be a real struggle. It seems to be extremely difficult to live in the moment, to "hang loose" and enjoy ourselves and others, let alone God. Yet to be light and salt in this world, especially when you are

22. This is why so many outsiders accuse Christians of Platonism. (One thinks of Nietzsche's accusation of Christianity as "Platonism for the people"). Platonism means that one is more interested in the world of ideas than the world of appearances, and the world of appearances is this world, where things change, where things do not work perfectly, where matter is stubborn. In the terms we have just been discussing, it is the world where people do what they do, even if they are foggy, or plainly disagree with you, about questions of purpose or destiny.

called to this task in the university, requires nothing less. Who said incarnational humanism, heeding Christ's call for the restoration of humanity to God, would be easy? It demands all of your effort and all of you, including your mind. - cliché

Study Questions

1. What have non-Christians ever done for you?
2. In what ways are Christians agents of common grace? In what ways are Christians recipients of common grace?
3. Why does C. S. Lewis argue that Christianity brought no new ethical code into the world?
4. According to Taylor, how does the great human tradition benefit from secular institutions? According to Newbigin, why can Christians join hands with people of other faiths and ideologies?

12

CONCLUSION

THIS BOOK BEGAN BY DEFENDING your suitability as a Christian student for university education. It showed how Christians played a determinative role in the development of humanism, which finds its natural home in the university. It has encouraged you to affirm various aspects of humanism, many of which arise from within Christianity and some of which were promoted by modern secularist culture but represent authentic developments of the gospel nonetheless. It has urged you not to repeat or be defeated by the error of dualism but rather to recognize that the incarnation affirms both what it means to be human and the irreducible necessity of transcendence—dependency on God—for the full flourishing of human existence.

Undeniably, we have asked you to work hard to understand the multi-stranded story of Christian thought and university humanism. It is incumbent upon the Christian student to immerse him- or herself in the tradition, the memory, the community of the church, the resources of humanism, and to apply Christian principles with discernment and openness to the perspectives of others. Practically speaking, in the context of university education, our argument means that the Christian student ought to affirm common grace. In the life of the mind, expectancy is everything.

We conclude by urging you to pursue your present university education in light of the following maxims.

Integration

Strive for integration as a Christian. Never separate faith from learning. Constantly challenge dualistic thinking that would marginalize religion or encapsulate spirituality in a bubble. In a secular institution you will receive very little help in this regard. If you are in one, presumably you have acknowledged and accepted this challenge. But you will not find yourself utterly alone. Recognize the constant need for intellectual community; you will find yourself in some community and ideology whether you like it or not. Demand of your local church genuine support, not merely unengaged platitudes or the trite warnings of the tremulous.

If you have chosen a Christian institution, you cannot assume that you have Christian integration covered. For one thing, it is not something someone else can do for you. It is not a commodity you can buy, however eagerly Christian universities brand themselves as selling it. Expect your professors to model integration, and engage them on this vital component. Christian integration indicates an awareness, on the instructor's part, of her or his own situatedness of teaching the subject matter from a specific and limited perspective. First, Christian integration indicates a posture of humility. Second, at its best, the phrase shows the instructor's commitment to raising issues of perspective in the classroom, educating students in the reality of interpretation and the limitations of rationality. Third, it evinces the educator's commitment to making sense of the data of a course in terms of, and with reference to, the larger Christian story of human purposes. This requires more than praying before class or sprinkling Bible verses throughout a lecture.

Christian integration demands from you no less than from the professor the thinking through of the entire material in light of the Christian story. There is no other way of scholarship if indeed all things are centered in Christ. The German theologian Dietrich Bonhoeffer has expressed this important idea most emphatically:

> There are, however, not two realms . . . but only one realm of
> Christ-reality, in which the profane and sacred realities are unified.
> Not two competing spheres coexist which contend with each other
> about their limits, so that the question of boundaries [between
> the sacred and the profane] becomes central to history; rather, the
> entire world reality is already taken up into Christ and from this
> center and towards this center does history move.[1]

The incarnation does not allow us to partition reality into spiritual
and nonspiritual spheres but shows that all reality and all truth
flow from one integrative source.

The phrase "Christian integration" needs to be handled with
great care so as not to suggest an attitude of arrogant omniscience.
It very easily conveys the basic assumption that Christians already
know the main outlines of the structure of human learning and
that what happens when we learn things is to fill in the details. It
is not at all clear, however, how most things one learns at a university fit into any particular worldview and why they cannot be
accommodated to several. For instance, the emphasis on collective
identity that one finds in the writings of Marx proved jarring to
most Christians in the late nineteenth and early twentieth centuries,
but on careful reflection many Christians have come to appreciate
the way in which socialism counterbalances an overemphasis on
individual rights in modern society. They have been able to find
parallels with biblical and prophetic warnings to care for the community. Furthermore, the analysis of factory conditions by Marx
and Engels provided an enormously important wake-up call to
many people to address the unbridled greed of early capitalists.
The spirit of that critique remains as pertinent today.

Christian integration cannot filter out information prematurely
on the grounds that, on the face of it, the information challenges
things that "must" be true from a Christian perspective. Very few
Christian thinkers will suppress facts. But what they are more
tempted to do is to dismiss ideas as false interpretations gener-
ated by an erroneous worldview. Here we need a great deal of
humility and circumspection. Such humility in no way implies that
the Christian has to embrace "metanarrative relativism," as if all
grand stories were of the same value. This erroneous conclusion
is one of the dehumanizing tendencies of postmodern culture,

1. Dietrich Bonhoeffer, *Ethics* (New York: Touchstone, 1995), 44.

which denies that all stories, including its own denial of such stories, are told with a universal intent. The Christian story is indeed exclusive in its universalism by its proclamation of Christ as Lord over all creation. Yet this truth in no way obviates the Christian's historical situatedness and hence limited, perspectival perception of truth.

Your Christian integration, as applied to any subject matter, ought to recognize explicitly the points on which Christians themselves are deeply divided. The phrase "Christian integration" can easily and tacitly imply that "all right-thinking Christians believe . . ." Perhaps more than anything, this tacit dimension of "Christian integration" militates against university education's goal of fostering a cast of mind that questions unstated assumptions. Are there others in the universal church who see the benefits of a given teaching that is prevalent in the broader university culture? This is certainly true of Marxist thought. It is also true of evolutionary theory. And of gene technology. And of whether we need to defend certain authors and artists as Christian in any meaningful sense. The list goes on. The story of Jesus unites us; where there is diversity in the church regarding the viability of certain ideas or discoveries, students would do well to recognize these disagreements as limiting the integration they should attempt. University education, never mind Christian charity, requires that we appreciate the diversity within our unity.

Of course, non-Christians are guilty of the same filtering process, often more so. One of the purposes of this book is to heighten the awareness that *everyone* faces the challenge of interpretation. There is no question of not filtering. Here we simply want to point out that Christians are not immune and that the phrase "Christian integration" can provide a cloak for an activity that needs to be undertaken with great care. Christians, in fact, should be better at resisting the temptation to filter out information that we cannot make sense of. The Christian virtues of humility and honesty compel us. So too does our familiarity with mystery, which profoundly marks the doctrines crucial to our story. There is simply a great deal we do not know or understand; part of our joy stems from realizing that these limitations cannot threaten us.

Integration can imply an attempt to make sense of all the data at a given time. Like the filtering process, the effort to synthesize knowledge is extremely important and deeply human. We are pattern-making creatures, making sense of the information we have at our disposal. We have an obligation, however, to recognize how very provisional our models must be. We never have all the available data at our fingertips at any given moment, and new insights are occurring all the time. Integration needs to have a "sell by" date imprinted on it. What models work best for now, in our present circumstances, given the current state of knowledge, the cultural milieu, and the political situation? Christian integration can easily slip into a timeless mode, but Christians have an obligation to appreciate the practical dimension of wisdom and not to divorce this from the academic enterprise.

Interdisciplinarity

Demand interdisciplinarity from your education. Interdisciplinarity used to be more natural as part of a broad-based liberal arts education, an educational approach that implied that one would receive at least some exposure to music, art, languages, the natural sciences, and the humanities. Zeal for relevance, practical applicability, and the misleading notion that expertise equals blinkered specialization have all put liberal arts education under grave threat.

This does not mean that you should opt for a university that sells a nostalgic vision of liberal arts education. Interdisciplinarity needs to be filtered through the demands of postmodernism, which have rightly dismantled many unquestioned assumptions of secular scientific humanism. Yet interdisciplinarity certainly needs to be engaged in ways that technical schools simply do not encourage. If worldviews govern our lives, we cannot simply stick our heads in the sand and work innocently in our narrowly defined disciplines. It is important to maintain an interdisciplinary outlook in order to understand the various shaping influences on our world.

As a student, one faces many pressures to decide on a pathway in life, to aim for a career, choose a major. These are important and necessary choices, and university education is becoming so expensive that one wants to get it right sooner rather than later. Specialization, however, inevitably means sacrificing important and related possibilities. This can happen by default, or one can think carefully about how to incorporate diverging or seemingly borderland intellectual interests into one's chosen area of study. This is increasingly what students are doing. Such a trend is not a mere luxury some can afford and others have to forego in light of obtaining a job. The emergent consensus among scholars is that the complexity of reality and our human involvement in understanding it *requires* interdisciplinarity.

Note that integration and interdisciplinarity are not the same thing. Interdisciplinarity requires a serious attempt to obtain the knowledge of another discipline. If integration is the acknowledgment of the need to bring things together, interdisciplinarity is the recognition that there will always be other perspectives and detailed knowledge that we cannot fully account for.

You Are a Student, Not a Client

Consider again the implications of the trend in university education toward trying to cater to your needs. Does the university acknowledge its responsibility to provide a sense of the ends to which it provides its training? If not, it has succumbed to the pressure to provide for its clients' material self-interests and given up its mandate to provide guidance and an interpretive framework. Without a sense of story that allows us to study with a basic sense of a universally acknowledgable purpose, the modern university merely reinforces disciplinary and intellectual fragmentation. The multiversity lacks a common purpose, which also explains its current form, the managerial university, with students as clients and professors as the bartenders who are expected to mix the desired cocktails and serve them to satisfaction.

You should not desire a university education constructed on such a model. Already the near universal concern about grade inflation in North American educational institutions indicates the familiar consumerist attitude: payment for education should guarantee satisfaction, even if this means complete self-delusion. The first-year student's expectancy to receive A's and B's on every assignment contradicts any notion of intellectual growth and the application of other intellectual criteria besides getting the facts straight—a criterion the student can validate for himself. Students (and the markers who surrender to grade inflation) apparently do not realize that this consumerist attitude directly contradicts the idea of education as an intellectual journey toward maturity. And yet, like the average consumer, students receive their inflated grades with the same delusional excitement we all feel for the great deal we brought home from Wal-Mart, only to see it break down a few months later.

While interdisciplinarity is crucial, offering an ever greater array of courses demanded by our fast-changing culture undermines the traditional mandate of the university to provide a unifying principle for meaningful career choices. Let us be clear: the university should respond to these needs, but this is not the heart of the university. If it were, technical schools could easily replace universities. Technical schools are by nature multiversities that supply job skills. The only unifying factor of technically oriented institutions is material advancement.[2] The liberal arts *university*, however, stands apart because it assumes and operates under an overall purpose that allows the student to integrate acquired skills toward a universally acknowledged goal of character formation and of growth into a greater understanding of what it means to be human. Put differently, the heart of the university is still humanism. When the university loses the idea of this ultimate purpose, it ceases to be a university. The label "technical university" is an oxymoron.

2. Worldview questions are, of course, being answered at postsecondary institutions other than universities, such as technical schools, but with far less opportunity given for students to reflect on the questions as part of their formal education. A university differs from a technical training institute in that the mandate of the technical institute is to train an individual to be able to do a particular task effectively, whether this task is to write computer programs or to inspect houses. The aim is to provide individuals with specific tools that make them immediately useful to society and employers. It is tempting to say that most people who go to a technical school do so to make themselves more immediately employable; utility is easily measured in terms of earning potential. Many, however, take technical courses to fulfill a personal ambition because they imagine obtaining considerable satisfaction out of being able to do such-and-such. Nonetheless, the objective in both instances is the same: equipping the individual with the skills to perform a given set of tasks. There need not be much difference between a university and a technical institute. Medicine, for instance, can be very much like technical training, merely one of its most prestigious forms. Seminaries, too, though often highly advanced in terms of their openness to "worldview thinking," are explicitly oriented toward training in a way that distinguishes them from universities. But the university is recognized to be the home of such reflection regardless of the pressures that have been put on it (and its students). Wherever fundamental, far-reaching, and holistic questions come from, there we call the home of the liberal arts and of humanistic university education.

At the current rate, Christian universities appear to be following their secular counterparts by promoting the client model under the guise of a focus on "student life" and "student-centered outcomes." This dualistic separation of the academic and spiritual dimensions of education not only confirms an already existing faith/reason split in the new student but also conveniently supports a university model in which the now split personality of the student is serviced by experts in each area. Often student life and university chapel, prayer meetings and spiritual retreats are completely severed from the academic branch of the university. Given the understanding of university we have developed here, this is entirely the wrong picture. Academic life should be the tree, and so-called spiritual retreats and exercises the branches that grow out of this tree. All university endeavors must be directed by this academic interest (rightly understood). It is only when we fall into the dualistic trap of disassociating academia from "real life out there" and from the spiritual-moral dimension of our existence that an actual division between a "holistic" or "student life" emphasis, on the one hand, and academic interests, on the other, becomes possible.

The university is primarily an academic enterprise. It guards an understanding of the state of knowledge in individual disciplines and continually updates this understanding. Through interdisciplinarity and integration, it scrutinizes various modes of knowing and applies cross-pollination to the self-critique of any one mode of knowing. It does this fully aware that if it does not maintain its own standards, others will import from elsewhere their own criteria for what counts as knowledge, whether on a business, technical, or "spiritual" model, to name just three possibilities. As we have tried to show, only a dualistic mind-set would separate academics from moral-spiritual development.

Humanism has always been concerned with self-knowledge and moral-spiritual development to produce intelligent leaders and shapers of culture. It is crucial for students to see that learning is spiritual development. Learning in itself is already a holistic experience. We would do well to recover this vision from the medieval era for our dualistic culture. Such learning never ends—it is a pilgrimage. During the economic upheavals, technological changes, and new realities of the 1990s, President Clinton observed that one of the most valuable assets university graduates possessed was having learned how to learn. Gone are the modernist presumptions of how life ought to unfold, assumptions related to male dominance, the socioeconomic make-up of our local environment, and our place in the world, either as individuals or as whole nations. Where once most students looked on university education as their ticket preparing them to take their places in this world, now we realize that university education prepares us to be able to adapt to changing places.

A university education worthy of the name prepares students for life's difficulties and inspires them with its enchanting possibilities. It is intensely oriented toward the practical life; ivory towers have a place in life, but they are neither the sum total of the university nor what it most prizes. The overall goal of the university education is the call to be most fully human. It can hope to achieve this goal only by embracing the incarnation.

Thinking Is Not Optional; It Is Part of Your Christian Identity

Students of faith encounter the transition to university life in a unique way, in the form of a challenge to their faith. Some have the mistaken idea that a Christian university will protect them from doubts and related assaults on their faith. Sometimes anxious parents and administrators express shock and dismay that a young person could express serious doubts or lose his or her faith after a term or two. This would be shocking only if the student came to the university with a perfect theology. But none of us has such a theology. All of us are on a journey, and our spiritual and intellectual life are bound up together. It may very well be the case that a student has satisfied himself or herself with a faith that the student has never really owned. Such a faith will crumble easily in the face of the impressive, carefully thought-through convictions of thinkers encountered at the university.

In an Eastern story, a seeker after truth visits a wise man living in a mountain hermitage and finds him meditating beside a mountain pool. When he asks the wise man what he must do to acquire truth, the wise man asks him to gaze into the water, then promptly grabs the seeker and holds his head under water for what seems like an eternity. Yanking the seeker's head out of the water, the hermit tells him, "You need to want the truth more than your next breath." Students, Christian or otherwise, do not usually arrive at a university with such an attitude; it is very easy for them and for others to interpret their intellectual experience as too difficult or threatening when they are confronted with concepts not easily assimilated or rebutted. In an age when we are invited to call students clients, it is tempting to put so much stock in their responses that we forget about the nature of a relationship in which both teacher and student are pilgrims and the teacher has more experience of the intractability of truth. The very moments when a professor may seem most demanding and the material most disturbing may be the very moments when the educational experience is most authentic, most shared. It may be a precious time of considerable vulnerability.

Yet this challenge to one's deepest assumptions plays an important part for the renewal of the mind and for the training of intelligent—indeed, wise—leaders for the coming generations. Christian education is not faith-affirming if it merely confirms our cultural and denominational prejudices. Only when our deepest assumptions are challenged will we be able to hold our faith with the kind of intelligent conviction that makes us credible witnesses of the new humanity instituted by Christ.

Because God has given all of us reason as a gift integral to understanding the world and our purpose in it, thinking is a Christian calling. In this calling the Christian has to recognize that reason is given to *all* and that *all truth* is God's truth, whether it comes from Heidegger, Julian of Norwich, or the apostle Paul. It is true that Jesus's answer to Pilate's all-important question "What is truth?" (an answer given to the disciples, though not to Pilate) still stands: "I am the way and the truth and the life. No one comes to the Father but by me."[3] But if Jesus is the incarnate Logos in whom we live, move, and have our being, then all truth is part of him and leads to him. This makes all truth about humanity and nature worthy of study.

To think is not a luxury for the Christian but part of the essence of the Christian's religion. We often forget that the apostle Paul's injunction to renew our minds includes an admonishment to critical reflection. You do not have to read Paul very long to find out that the heart of his theology is the continual working

3. John 14:6.

out of a new vision for human life after the events of the incarnation, the cross, and the resurrection. In every one of his letters, Paul expresses his frustration with the church's failure to reflect critically on its cultural practices in light of the incarnation. In this respect at least, the track record of Christian universities matches that of the church.

Traditionally, Christians have been well aware of the need for critical reflection and have acknowledged that genuine thinking is agony. Students need to embrace this aspect of obtaining a degree. Wrestling with foundational questions is hard work, a continual hermeneutical process of learning facts, concepts, and ideas within shifting frameworks of interpretation. We return to the thought of C. S. Lewis, who appreciated the demand that education puts on the Christian student.

Lewis was mindful of the hermeneutical dynamic in education. In *The Screwtape Letters*, Screwtape explains it as "the law of undulation":

> Humans are amphibians—half spirit and half animal. (The Enemy's determination to produce such a revolting hybrid was one of the things that determined Our Father to withdraw his support from Him.) As spirits they belong to the eternal world, but as animals they inhabit time. This means that while their spirit can be directed to an eternal object, their bodies, passions, and imaginations are in continual change, for to be in time means to change. Their nearest approach to constancy, therefore, is undulation—the repeated return to a level from which they repeatedly fall back, a series of troughs and peaks.[4]

The context for these remarks is his nephew's error in failing to keep a human from converting to Christianity. Screwtape finds solace in this law of undulation, the movement from initial enthusiasm for an idea or project to the inevitable disappointment when the work begins. He advises his nephew to play on this natural dynamic to disenchant the new convert to Christianity:

> Work hard, then, on the disappointment or anticlimax which is certainly coming to the patient during his first few weeks as a churchman. The Enemy allows this disappointment to occur on

4. C. S. Lewis, *The Screwtape Letters* (New York: Macmillan, 1943), 44.

the threshold of every human endeavour. It occurs when the boy
who has been enchanted in the nursery by *Stories from the Odyssey*
buckles down to really learning Greek. It occurs when lovers have
got married and begin the real task of learning to live together.
In every department of life it marks the transition from dreaming
aspiration to laborious doing.[5]

What is true of moving from *Stories from the Odyssey* to learning Greek is equally true of all aspects of university education.
It is vital to remember what enchanted you and attracted you to
your chosen major in the first place; we never cease to need the
reminders of what we glimpsed initially, what offered the promise
of stimulation for the life of the mind. At the same time, we need
to brace ourselves for the difficult task of mastering a subject.

One should not miss the significance of Lewis's main point here:
learning and thinking are hard work not only because they exercise
our intellectual muscles but because of learning's existential dimensions. What the Christian calls faith (trust in God) is not so dissimilar
from what the non-Christian might call trust in principles or ultimate
convictions. Real thinking always challenges these faiths, or basic
beliefs; this makes genuine critical reflection so painful.

When was the last time you reflected on life's difficulty, or the
challenge an academic subject presents to your faith, as an indication of God's love? The devil, at least, understands this possible
linkage. Screwtape explains that the Enemy (God) allows for undulation to encourage his followers in choosing him on the basis
of their own free wills. The devil again:

> He really *does* want to fill the universe with a lot of loathsome little
> replicas of Himself—creatures whose life, on its miniature scale,
> will be qualitatively like His own, not because He has absorbed
> them but because their wills freely conform to His. . . . Merely to
> override a human will (as His felt presence in any but the faintest
> and most mitigated degree would certainly do) would be for Him
> useless. He cannot ravish. He can only woo. For His ignoble idea
> is to eat the cake and have it; the creatures are to be one with Him,
> but yet themselves; merely to cancel them, or assimilate them, will
> not serve.[6]

5. Ibid., 17.
6. Ibid., 45–46.

Lewis's perspective on the aim of the religious life conflicts with the view that faith debilitates philosophical inquiry or that faith can do without learning. A person's experience of freedom, including the freedom of intellectual inquiry, is absolutely fundamental to authentic Christian experience.[7] Thinking, with all its risks, is mandatory for the Christian.

Conclusion

Thomas Aquinas understood well the divine calling to critical thinking with all its risks, which is why he embraced it in humility and trust. He realized that God is not interested in mindless slaves but in responsible sons and daughters who are not swayed easily by every cultural change or intellectual fad but whose faith seeks understanding and who therefore embrace the risk of deep critical reflection necessitated by their conversion to Christianity. With Aquinas, we should honor our Lord by struggling against the "double darkness" occasioned by "sin and ignorance." As you will see in the following prayer, Aquinas understood that education is both intellectual and spiritual, a faith that seeks understanding. This is not a bad place to begin as a student as you embark on your university education or as you embark on your day:

> Creator of all things, true source of light and wisdom,
> origin of all being,
> graciously let a ray of your light penetrate
> the darkness of my understanding.
> Take from me the double darkness
> in which I have been born,
> an obscurity of sin and ignorance.
> Give me a keen understanding,
> a retentive memory, and
> the ability to grasp things correctly and fundamentally.
> Grant me the talent of being exact
> in my explanations and the ability to express myself

7. Indeed, contrary to Critchley's earlier assumption that Christians do not know the agony of radical thought, we could argue that the Christian's stakes are incomparably higher because a challenge to the Christian's fundamental convictions strikes not only at an idea but at a personal relation that never has the apodicticity an abstractly held concept may appear to grant us.

with thoroughness and charm.
Point out the beginning,
direct the progress,
and help in the completion.
I ask this through Christ our Lord.
Amen.

Study Questions

1. What is integration? How does it differ from interdisciplinarity?
2. According to incarnational humanism, why is the model of the student as client inadequate for university education?
3. In what sense is the academic enterprise spiritual? In what sense is it vocational, in the full Christian sense of that term?
4. Now that you have read through the book, how would you reply to the charge that Christians cannot think?
5. Discuss an occasion in which you have experienced the agony of thought as an expression of your freedom in Christ and an indication of God's love and grace.

SUGGESTED FURTHER READING

W E HIGHLY RECOMMEND THAT YOU follow up on the footnotes. The works cited there help provide a good introductory picture of the history of the university and its current challenges. The following is a list of further reading on select topics.

History and Development of the University

For a general overview of the medieval foundations of the university, C. H. Haskins, *The Rise of Universities* (Ithaca, NY: Cornell University Press, 1965), and Hastings Rashdall, *The Universities of Europe in the Middle Ages*, ed. F. M. Powicke and A. B. Emden, new ed., 3 vols. (New York: Oxford University Press, 1987), though old, are still useful. If you want to delve deeply into the history of the university, we recommend the meticulously researched series *A History of the University in Europe*, under the general editorship of Walter Rüegg (New York: Cambridge University Press, 1992–). R. W. Southern's writings are very important, especially his multivolume magnum opus *Scholastic Humanism and the Unification of Europe* (Cambridge, MA: Blackwell, 1995–). He gives a good sense of the interconnectedness of humanism, the university, and sociocultural developments.

Medieval Humanism

The most exhaustive treatment of this topic appears in R. W. Southern's books. Historians of science now look to figures wrestling with naturalistic aspects of inquiry in the thirteenth century as making an important contribution to the development of modern empirical science. For a brief general discussion of the stages of scientific development, see Alistair C. Crombie, "Science and the Arts in the Renaissance: The Search for Truth and Certainty, Old and New," in *Science and the Arts in the Renaissance,* ed. John W. Shirley and F. David Hoeniger (Washington: The Folger Shakespeare Library, 1985), 15–26. See also David C. Lindberg and Ronald L. Numbers, eds., *God and Nature: Historical Essays on the Encounter between Christianity and Science* (Berkeley: University of California Press, 1986). For medieval interest in the subjects of light and sight in particular, see David Lindberg, *Theories of Optics from al-Kindi to Kepler* (Chicago: University of Chicago Press, 1976); Bruce Eastwood, "Medieval

Empiricism: The Case of Grosseteste's Optics," *Speculum* 43 (1968), 306–21. This fascination with natural aspects, notably in terms of light and sight, extended to the arts as well, with writers applying aspects of this learning to such cultural phenomena as courtly love. At the same time, inquiry retained a vital interest in spiritual dimensions.

The medieval theologian Thomas Aquinas is the best example of holistic medieval humanism. Start with Thomas Aquinas, *Aquinas on Nature and Grace*, ed. A. M. Fairweather (Philadelphia: Westminster Press, 1954). A good introduction to Thomas's life and thought is G. K. Chesterton's biographical sketch *St. Thomas Aquinas* (New York: Sheed & Ward, 1933; repr., New York: Image, 1956). Josef Pieper also makes Thomas very accessible in his *Guide to Thomas Aquinas*, trans. Richard and Clara Winston (New York: New American Library, 1962). See also Anthony Kenny, *Aquinas* (Oxford: Oxford University Press, 1980). For insights into medieval humanism through the lens of the experience of Abelard and Heloise, see Étienne Gilson, *Heloise and Abelard* (Ann Arbor: University of Michigan Press, 1960).

Literary Humanism

The anthology *English Humanism: Wyatt to Cowley*, ed. Joanna Martindale (Dover, NH: Croom Helm, 1985), provides a fine selection of humanistic topics and concerns. For a deeper understanding of this movement, consult the primary texts of Erasmus of Rotterdam (particularly *Enchiridion* in vol. 66 of *Collected Works of Erasmus* [Toronto: University of Toronto Press, 1988]) and Thomas More (his best-known work is *Utopia* [New York: Cambridge University Press, 2002]); see also More's letters, particularly those written to his daughter from prison (*The Last Letters of Thomas More*, ed. Alvaro de Silva [Grand Rapids: Eerdmans, 2000]). The Italian thinker Giambattista Vico is an extension of this literary humanism. His writings are rather difficult, but a very faithful interpretation of Vico appears in Isaiah Berlin, *Three Critics of the Enlightenment: Vico, Hamann, Herder*, ed. Henry Hardy (Princeton, NJ: Princeton University Press, 2000), which also contains a good summary of Enlightenment ideals and the counterarguments of contemporaries to this movement.

Enlightenment Humanism

The best way to deepen your understanding of Enlightenment thinkers is to read primary sources. Kant's small but compact essay "An Answer to the Question, 'What Is Enlightenment?'" will make a good start. But a full grasp of the various ideas and concepts requires wide reading. The German, English, and French Enlightenment thinkers are not all of the same opinion. French thinkers such as Voltaire, for example, were much more antagonistic to Christianity than a German Enlightenment figure such as Lessing. *What Is Enlightenment? Eighteenth-Century Answers and Twentieth-Century Questions*, ed. James Schmidt (Berkeley: University of California Press, 1996), contains a reasonable selection of primary Enlightenment texts with current reflection on their importance.

Scientific Secular Humanism

Descartes and Bacon are important, even iconic figures in the rise of scientific objectivism. Francis Bacon's *Advancement of Learning, Novum Organum, and New Atlantis*, all available in various editions, make excellent reading, as does René Descartes's *Medita-*

tions on First Philosophy, trans. Donald A. Cress (Indianapolis: Hackett, 1979). A very good essay on this development and how it affected the university is Isaiah Berlin, "The Divorce between the Sciences and the Humanities," in Berlin, *The Proper Study of Mankind: An Anthology of Essays*, ed. Henry Hardy and Roger Hausheer (London: Pimlico, 1998), 326–58. Another source is Thomas Sprat, *History of the Royal Society* (1667), ed. Jackson I. Cope and Harold Whitmore Jones (St. Louis: Washington University Press, 1958).

Post-Enlightenment Humanism

For an overview of the rise of the Enlightenment and the attendant problems of modernity, Charles Taylor, *Malaise of Modernity* (Cambridge: Harvard University Press/Toronto: Anansi, 1991), first given as a series of public lectures, makes excellent reading. Probably the most readable and most widely known secular philosopher we have discussed is Friedrich Nietzsche. *The Birth of Tragedy*, trans. Walter Kaufmann (New York: Vintage Books, 1967), and *The Gay Science*, trans. Walter Kaufmann (New York: Random House, 1974), give a good sense of his criticisms both of the Enlightenment and of Christianity. Graham Good, *Humanism Betrayed: Theory, Ideology, and Culture in the Contemporary University* (Montreal and Ithaca, NY: McGill-Queen's University Press, 2001), conveys a sense of the anxiety many feel about the contemporary university from the vantage point of a secular academic. For a different, though still secular, approach to contemporary intellectual questions, Simon Critchley's little book *On Humour* (New York: Routledge, 2002) provides a good example of the pos-

ture he would have us all take to the challenge of being human.

Postmodernism

Sympathizers and adherents usually write the best introductions to postmodernism. Christian assessments are often mere caricatures with unhelpful blanket statements. For a solid understanding of deconstruction, Simon Critchley, *The Ethics of Deconstruction: Derrida and Levinas*, 2nd ed. (West Lafayette, IN: Purdue University Press, 1999), merits a high recommendation. Richard Kearney, *States of Mind* (New York: New York University Press, 1995), which contains interviews with key postmodern thinkers who state in a very conversational tone the reasons for their claims, is also excellent; the interview with Levinas is particularly good.

Reading Gadamer or Heidegger demands time and patience. Gadamer's essays collected in *Reason in the Age of Science*, trans. Frederick G. Lawrence (Cambridge, MA: MIT Press, 1995), and *Philosophical Hermeneutics,* ed. and trans. David. E. Linge (Berkeley: University of California Press, 1976), are recommended.

Heidegger is most accessible in his lectures. Instead of beginning with *Being and Time*, start with *The Fundamental Concepts of Metaphysics: World, Finitude, Solitude*, trans. William McNeill and Nicholas Walker (Bloomington: Indiana University Press, 1996), which is much more accessible and is considered by many as important as *Being and Time*. For determining what postmodernism means to you as a Christian, a helpful book is Robert Greer, *Mapping Postmodernism: A Survey of Christian Options* (Downers Grove, IL: InterVarsity, 2003). Greer explains the different postmodern positions and discusses how they may or may not be compatible with Christian faith, without, however, claiming that the Christian has everything figured out. A detailed account of Gadamer's and Levinas's thinking and their compatibility with Christian theology appears in Jens Zimmermann, *Recovering Theological Hermeneutics* (Grand Rapids: Baker Academic), 2004.

Incarnational Humanism

N. T. Wright, "The Light of the World," chapter 8 in *The Challenge of Jesus* (Downers Grove, IL: InterVarsity, 1999), which summarizes well Wright's notion of a new humanity in Christ, is a good starting point for further study of what we have called incarnational humanism. Other contemporary theologians encourage a proper sense of how the Christian is to live eschatologically—fully in this world but enacting the already come and yet coming kingdom. A very good beginning for the study of Dietrich Bonhoeffer is his *Letters from Prison* (New York: Touchstone, 1997) rather than *Discipleship* (also called *The Cost of Discipleship*) (Minneapolis: Fortress, 2001); read also his *Ethics* (Minneapolis: Fortress, 2004). For Hans-Urs von Balthasar, a good introduction is his *Explorations in Theology*, 4 vols. (San Francisco: Ignatius, 1989). A pertinent contemporary theologian is Rowan Williams. One might start with the collection of his sermons and talks published as *A Ray of Darkness* (Cambridge, MA: Cowley, 1995) (also published as *Open to Judgement* [London: Darton, Long-

man & Todd, 1994]). For his views on how specific individuals in the Christian tradition from New Testament times through the Reformation wrestled with a spirituality that embodies incarnational humanism, see *The Wound of Knowledge*, 2nd rev. ed. (Cambridge, MA: Cowley, 1991) (1st ed. published as *Christian Spirituality* [Atlanta: John Knox, 1980]).

The Christian University

The extensive literature on this topic is often permeated with an anxiety that Christian colleges will eventually die unless they clamp down the dogmatic-denominational safety lid on dangerous humanistic tendencies. One of the best recent books on the Christian university and on learning in general is Nicholas Wolterstorff et al., *Educating for Shalom: Essays on Christian Higher Education* (Grand Rapids: Eerdmans, 2004). Wolterstorff advocates a Christian humanism along the lines suggested here. Two other excellent introductions to faith-based universities are Jaroslav Pelikan, *The Idea of the University: A Reexamination* (New Haven: Yale University Press, 1992), and the book it echoes, the classic nineteenth-century work (with the same title) by the Catholic theologian John Henry Newman, who also served as a university president: *The Idea of a University*, ed. Frank Turner (New Haven: Yale University Press, 1996). Various editions of this book are available, as are versions in electronic format on the Internet.

INDEX